ENDORSEMENTS

This book shares the undeniable truth that God is at work in the most minute details of our lives.

Judy Schwechten
Original Cofounder of Heart for the House

The Real Deal is a heart-to-heart conversation with a friend. Reading it, we are reminded that God sweetly pursues us right in the midst of our life's story! Kelly shares many stories of joy and sorrow while pointing us to the most authentic hope!

Kimberly Powers
Author & Speaker

The Real Deal is a compelling story of love. The love of an earthly father for his family as a reflection of our heavenly Father's love for humanity. God's love for us through Jesus Christ is "The Real Deal"!

Michael Legg
Church Leadership Mentor

THE
REAL
DEAL

LESSONS LEARNED FOR
LIVING AN AUTHENTIC LIFE

KELLY DOLAN EHLERS

Published by HigherLife Development Services Inc.
PO Box 623307
Oviedo, Florida 32762
www.ahigherlife.com

ISBN: 978-1-958211-69-4 paperback
ISBN: 978-1-958211-70-0 ebook
Library of Congress Control Number: 1-12808447301

Printed in the United States of America.
10 9 8 7 6 5 4 3 2 1

DEDICATION

This book is dedicated to my husband, who has been steadfast in his support of this project and in the hard work of taking care of my parents and beyond. His endurance during these years, right up to the present, amazes me. His consistent efforts to show grace and unrelenting love make an enduring impression on this humble soul.

I would be remiss not to thank my parents too. Although they are in heaven, their courage and unfailing love for God, each other, and others is what makes this story "the Real Deal." They would be thankful it's all about God working in and through every moment.

CONTENTS

ACKNOWLEDGMENTS

A heartfelt thank you to all those listed. You have given your time, prayers, and encouragement in order to see this book to fruition.

To Judy Schwechten, my mentor, dearest friend, and cofounder of HHM. Thank you for all the time and guidance you have given to me. Your initial edits of the rough draft made sure it revealed the truth of God's Word.

To Michael Legg, my mentor and friend. Thank you for getting me to the next steps early on in this journey. Your dedication to the Lord and encouragement urged me to take those next steps in obedience to God and to help bring this book to print.

To Kimberly Sweet Powers, thank you for always being there. Your love, prayers, and willingness to listen no matter the hour saw me through the most difficult of circumstances.

To all the women of HHM, specifically Dolores Gabriel-Ledbetter, Kimberly Hansin, and Holly King. Thank you for your friendship, steadfast love, and support during the many years of our study group and beyond.

To my core ladies, Cindy Renfrew, and Erin Sloan, thank you for your love, honesty, and continual support. May God bless us as we continue to grow in faith, hope, and love through Jesus Christ.

To the Spiro community group and brothers and sisters at Alive Church, thank you for your prayers, encouragement and doing life together. We are beyond blessed!

To all my family and extended family, thank you for your love and allowing me to tell my story.

To HigherLife, specifically Virginia Grounds, thank you for believing in this project and walking me through each step of the process. It has been a privilege to work with you.

To all the kids I've taught and mentored throughout the years. Each one of you and your stories matter! Continue to see where God is leading you no matter how you feel or the challenges you see. Remember, you can do all things through Christ who strengthens you (see Philippians 4:13).

To my husband, Jim, thank you for holding me and helping me to live.

To God, for continuous grace, love, and guidance.

INTRODUCTION

For the better part of my youth, I lived in a constant state of recurring anxiety, questioning, rebellion, and doubting. It started after a traumatic event where someone took my innocence at a young age. I never told anyone, not even my parents. I was scared and confused. Out of fear I just continued as if all were well, so much so it was one of the only times in my youth I had blocked and would not revisit until much later in life.

At age eleven, I found out that I had been adopted at birth. My parents were loving, yet after this revelation, there was always a nagging feeling that I was given up or unwanted. My parents tried to reinforce that I was special and chosen. I just started feeling that no matter how good something was it would not last. I remember going to the mall in my early teens and studying women to see who looked like me, wondering if one was my birth mother? We all search for authenticity, for identity, for realness, and truth.

During my late teens and twenties, the cycles of instability, anxiety, and indifference seemed to continue swirling even more rapidly. I was physically and mentally abused while in a long-term relationship. I excused all the toxic behavior because he had been severely beaten and abused as a child. I had no idea who I was anymore because I felt so broken. I finally left after the last traumatic event, but I needed help. I remember when a doctor who spent five minutes with me attempted to label me with bipolar disorder. I did not accept that diagnosis; it did not quite fit, and as life would have it another doctor debunked this and explained that I had PTSD. I identified with this diagnosis due to the actions and experiences that had brought me where I was in the first place.

Many times, during our search for truth, identity, and authenticity, people, some very educated, will put labels on you. Medical diagnoses and labels are meant for insurance purposes as well as to guide your care, which is something I didn't realize back then. Those labels may or may not be helpful or even true. But the one label you need to always remember is that you are "fearfully and wonderfully made" (Psa. 139:14). That is an authentic identity label!

Something happened which, although it did not transform my way of thinking right away, did have an eternal impact on my life. Someone led me to the Bible. A dear man, a former atheist, drunk, and rebel, sat down beside me along with his wife and kids and told me his story. He shared how he had found his black leather-bound Bible after pulling over on the side of the road following a long night of partying. He told me that this book was "the most powerful tool you can ever utilize." He and his wife shared their home, their life, and faith walk with me. I knew I wanted what they had; there was a peace and joy I had never really experienced, and it was authentic. Even though they shared with me the most vital component of their lives, I was not ready for the transformation. I thought it was much easier to ride the wave of insanity that I already knew than to get off and find a new balance on the one I was meant to ride.

So, here I am in my mid-fifties, and I can only tell you that the pages to follow will give you a glimpse into how I found authentic, real, honest, and power-filled living and how thankful I am. My hope is that you will figure it out too and that it does not take a sledgehammer, like it did for me, for you to realize all that is awaiting you. *The Real Deal* is for anyone who searches for authenticity, identity, and truth in their lives.

Authoring this book was not something I chose but a tangible effort of obedience to God. It has been a long, arduous journey and an incredibly special one. I remember sitting in my favorite chair at a Bible study, among encouraging ladies I adored, reiterating in my head all the reasons I could not write this book. Finally, the last excuse I could think of was, "I don't even have a title," thinking that would be the end of that. Quickly, three words were impressed in my heart that would be the title of this book and the beginning of this wonderful writing journey: The Real Deal. That evening is so clear to me now, and I chuckle at all the people and experiences along this journey that encouraged and pointed me in the right direction.

God sweetly pursues us, whether we are living within a Christian culture that shouts God's name or a pagan culture that embraces concepts foreign to Christianity. It is my understanding that in other countries, often God gives visions about Jesus Christ, since so many do not have the privilege of reading in a Bible about His sacrifice on the cross. Nor do they live in a culture that encourages finding universal truth and love. But God pursues us even in our Christian culture where we have His recorded Word. Perhaps the experiences I have recorded in my own life will help you to allow God to be the Lord of your life.

CHAPTER 1

THE FLOOR AND THE MOUNTAIN

The mountain is the place of deep connection with God, of instruction and strengthening. Our journeys to the mountain take many forms, but all begin at the same place, on our knees, on the floor.

I sat listening to the homily at our home church. Deacon Bubba was speaking about people going to the mountain and what it meant. I remembered that my dad had talked about this and knew I needed to pay close attention. In the Bible, going to the mountain signifies a spiritual journey. The journey to the mountain will include temptation, as it did for Jesus:

> Again, the devil took him to a high mountain and showed Jesus all the kingdoms of the world and their splendor.
>
> "All this I will give you," he said, "if you will bow down and worship me."

> Jesus said to him, "Away from me Satan! For it is written: 'Worship the Lord your God, and serve Him only.'" (Matthew 4:8–12)

Like Jesus, we can and should expect to be tempted on the mountain.

Scripture also shows us that to go to the mountain means to pray and to seek God:

> The Lord said, "I have indeed seen the misery of my people in Egypt. I have heard them crying out because of their slave drivers, and I am concerned about their suffering." (Exodus 3:7)

> Then we cried out to the Lord, the God of our ancestors, and the Lord heard our voice and saw our misery, toil, and oppression. So, the Lord brought us out of Egypt with a mighty hand and an outstretched arm, with great terror and with signs and wonders. (Deuteronomy 26:7–8)

It was on a mountain that God gave Moses the Ten Commandments (see Exodus 24:15). On numerous occasions, Jesus went out to a mountainside to pray (see Luke 6:12). He spent the night praying on the Mount of Olives prior to His arrest and journey to the cross (see Luke 22:39–46). My own journey to the mountain begins on one of the flattest terrains, the floor.

It was Christmas Eve, in the year 2000, and I was over five months pregnant. Upon entering my bedroom, I fell to my knees crying out to the Lord, asking Him to heal my dad. We had found out a few months before that he had stage IV lung and brain cancer and a death sentence. My heart broke open to the Lord and my prayers were real and raw in a way they had never been before. My longing for the Lord to hear my cry echoed David's entreaties in the Book of Psalms. I drenched my bed in tears and was worn out from my groaning.

> All night long I flood my bed with weeping and drench my couch with tears. (Psalm 6:6)

That evening I specifically asked God that He would allow my dad to stay on this earth long enough to have an impact on his yet unborn grandson. In addition, I asked God to take any stress of this challenging time off my shoulders so that my baby would not be affected by the emotional strain that grief and anxiety can bring on a body. The truth is, in the weeks prior to this Christmas Eve, I sobbed uncontrollably every night on my way home from my parents' house, at times wondering if it would be the last time I would see or talk to my dad. I could not bear the thought of losing him!

Not only did my specific and sincere heartfelt prayers get answered but I also came to a new level of understanding about prayer and how to pray. I had put my utmost trust and hope in God, which is His fervent desire for us. We say that when our children speak loving, trusting words to us, those words are like music to our ears. Our Father God's desire for conversation and relationship with us is that real. Our bare, specific, and devout prayers to God are like sweet music to Him. We are giving Him our heart's yearning.

Do you need to cry out to God about something specific? He is waiting!

You know prayer can happen anywhere! My experience is that the more consistent I am with prayer, the more I learn about who God really is. Prayer is one way to be continually in relationship with God and it is a two-way conversation that calls us to speak, but also to listen. Prayer is imperative because even though God already knows what we need and desire, we don't always know what God plans and desires. Prayer frees us up to allow God's thoughts and ways to become our thoughts and ways, to have the mind of Christ.

> Our bare, specific, and devout prayers to God are like sweet music to Him. We are giving Him our heart's yearning.

Prayer is our most authentic way to come to God. In prayer, we bring our reality into God's presence and receive His supernatural ability to bring the healing, peace, and comfort that nothing else can provide.

From the day I prayed for the miracle of allowing my dad to live and for the stress and anxiety of the illness to be taken off me, I was freed of that burden. A new peace permeated my being. I had prayed for peace and contentment before, but the prayers were "me-centered," not God-centered. Of course, I desired healing for my dad, but not for my benefit—for God to use him in my son's life.

After that evening my dad was miraculously given a full remission from his cancer. The doctors chalked up his remission as nothing short of a miracle, and I knew it was a miracle from God.

My father was at my son's birth and had many days of joyful occasions with our family. We enjoyed every extra moment he was given! We treasured these times and made many joy-filled memories. God had heard my cry and had seen fit to demonstrate His love and goodness in a wonderful way.

The day after my son Connor's second birthday, however, the "mountain" came to my daddy. My dad would have to submit his will and his desires to how God would allow His glory to shine. And I would be journeying to my own "mountain" again, on my knees, on the floor, increasingly praying.

I knew from the moment my mother called on the evening of April 28, 2003, that Dad's cancer had come back full force, but by now he had been in his grandson's life exactly two years. His influence was seen primarily in my son's eating habits. Connor knew when we would be at Grammy and Grampy's it was time to eat and enjoy tasty food and great company! Eat snacks, eat lunch, eat dinner, and yes, always eat dessert. There was a love for all kinds of wonderful food instilled in my son at an early age!

When we didn't have Grammy's wonderful home cooking, we were out at one of the local fresh seafood restaurants. Boy, did we ever have fun eating! To this day I know the food was good but more important was the quality of time spent with those we loved so dearly. These opportunities gave us a chance to sit back, breathe, and enjoy each other. We took in each moment, savoring each memory, as we took in the delicious flavors and textures of the foods we ate. We thanked God for much more than the food, for He was giving us this precious time to cherish.

That call from my mother came exactly one day after Connor turned two. My parents had been at our home the day before celebrating their grandson's birthday, and I could tell my dad was tired as we commemorated Connor's big day. It was a warm April day and Daddy was more winded than usual. Although he didn't grumble or complain, I could see something was wrong. As my mother spoke on the phone that evening, I heard the concern in her trembling voice and felt the unsteadiness that had become her companion in the last few years. The hospital had called my mom. My father was in the ER, and she needed me to go to the hospital.

My mother was unable to drive due to a disease called MSA, multiple system atrophy, a horrific disease that takes your most basic physical abilities to a whole new level of challenge. During her illness, with all its challenges, my mother did not complain. She honestly never whined about her condition or grumbled. Yes, she was a saint! My mom took every day and lived, lived the best she could! I loved her example of courage and grace, and I so desire to live like that—faithful and unshakable no matter what life throws your way or how unsteady you may feel physically.

My father was a truly kind man who would listen to anyone. He was a regular senior on the fast-food circuit in our hometown, and the staff at all the restaurants knew him by the name, Jack. Jack would meet friends daily, hang out, and eat. My dad enjoyed these friendships and loved life. He brought a smile to many and encouraged everyone he could. Many times, Dad would have a joke or a story to share. On this particular day, his trip to Burger King became the moment our lives would be changed forever, and my dad's journey to the mountain would begin.

That day he ate breakfast, drank coffee, had a conversation, and after an hour or so he went out to his car to return home. He sat there in the car. It was another sweltering day and there he sat in the car staring blankly ahead. I do not know how much time transpired, and I am thankful for the staff at Burger King. They knew him well enough that when he did not respond to their knocks on the window, they called the rescue squad.

After getting off the phone with my mother, I raced to meet my father in the emergency room, where he had been transported by ambulance. As I walked into the ER my daddy smiled tenderly and I smiled back, both of us knowing that it was time and that this day Dad's journey to the mountain began. The mountain in my dad's case would be his journey to submitting all to God, sacrificing everything to God's will, God's plan, and God's way even when it was not the way he, or we, wanted. His journey to the mountain became the bridge by which God showed us heaven.

My father shared lots of information with me during his illness; we talked for hours on end. He told me, "The doctor has said when the cancer comes back, it will come with a vengeance." That it would be painful was an understatement. And those words rang true. My father felt the physical pain of the cancer's return. My mother and family felt the intense emotional pain of watching our loved one slip away painfully. Our world would never be the same. And yet God increasingly made His presence known through the Holy Spirit as we progressed through this season together.

Though he suffered excruciating pain with every day that passed, my father had only one concern—the best for my mom's future. Up until that day I never quite understood the love they shared; I didn't understand the relationship they had. They had a love for each other that transcended every trouble attempting to knock them out. They were a team and no matter what happened in life they were there for each other. My mom and dad had a deeply-rooted faith in Jesus Christ that permeated how they lived their lives and how they raised their children.

They did not quote Scripture, but later I would see how scripturally sound their advice and guidance always were. We were raised in the Catholic Church, and never ever missed a Mass. We knew who led our family—God was always the center. Their responses to life's difficulties characterized what God calls us to in relationship with others, especially those whom we have vowed to love for life. My husband often reminds me, "We are on the same team." My parents were on the same team. I have a luxury not given to everyone, that of looking back and being thankful for my upbringing.

Do you feel that life is attempting to knock you out?

Have you been to the mountain or on the floor? Have you searched for God? He is there ever patiently awaiting your heart reaching out to Him. He desires to be in relationship with you and He has every good thing waiting. So, if you haven't been formally introduced, just say hello! God is real and closer than a friend! He will not fail you! Cry out to Him. He is the Real Deal!

CHAPTER 2

MY FATHER'S MOUNTAIN

After our emergency room visit, the next step for my father was seeing the oncologist. Going to the doctor with my dad was like going back in time, yet now the roles were reversed. I became the parent, and as much as it hurt, my parent now became the child. My mother was in a wheelchair, my dad weak, and I just wanted them both to be okay, healthy, and enjoying the retirement they had worked so hard to see. To this day I think of all the plans they had once they retired. This is not at all what they, or I, expected. And yet, they gracefully walked it out with a love and peace that was beyond understanding.

> We can make our plans, but the LORD determines our steps. (Proverbs 16:9 NLT)

This was when I stepped into a proactive mode, setting up an MRI to check Dad's brain for the return visit of this horrific disease. Oh, how the doctors wanted to postpone the scan and schedule us out a week. "No," I said. "No, we will be there today."

They scheduled us for that afternoon at the hospital. After dropping my mother back home so that she could rest, I took my dad to the hospital for his MRI. Thank you, God, for giving me the voice! I have not ever had that voice for myself, but for others, especially my parents, I was prepared to advocate in every way possible.

The following day we had an appointment with the doctor to review the MRI results. They showed that my dad's cancer was back and that once again it was in his brain. They would not be able to treat as invasively as before, due to the earlier chemotherapy and radiation, but they would attempt to slow down the cancer. The doctor gently told us that Dad might have as long as six months or as little as two weeks. We would have to wait and see. More importantly, it was on this day that God's revelations would begin.

On our short ride home from the hospital my dad fell asleep, which he always could do very easily. As a night shift guard, he could sleep day or night if he wasn't on duty. When I woke him, he said, "Let me climb the mountain! I can't get to the top, Kelly." Let's just say that this would certainly not be the last time my dad would say he was climbing the mountain and that he couldn't get to the top.

He began to share with me that there were two ladies in line behind him going up this mountain. These ladies told him they would have to go before him. Was God perhaps revealing truth about the journey my dad was taking? I felt compelled to pay extra attention to the details that my father was sharing, and so began my own journey.

> There is a time for everything, and
> a season for every activity under the
> heavens. (Ecclesiastes 3:1)

Some would say the following incident was a coincidence, but as I returned to work the following day a fellow teacher told me her grandmother had gone on to see the Lord the evening before, and in addition another close friend of her family had passed. Every hair on my body stood up and I thought of the two ladies my dad had said needed to go first to the mountain. I asked if her grandmother and family friend had known Jesus. She confirmed that yes, they had both known the Lord. They had known Jesus as their Lord and Savior. What a relief to know this about our loved ones! I encouraged my friend that she would see her grandmother again and told her about my dad's dream.

This was the same day my boss approached me about taking so much time off to take care of my family. I started that very evening filling out the paperwork for family medical leave in order to be prepared for full-time caregiving for my dad and mom on this journey.

Now this was the beginning of May and for a week or so I would drive forty-five minutes to my parents' home after work, then thirty minutes home after I had gotten their dinner and Dad settled for the night. Then straight to work again the next morning, then to my parents.... After we received the results of the MRI and the progression of my dad's condition I stayed with my parents. Taking care of them, especially my father, became my full-time job and it was the sweetest blessing. And yet it was wrapped in the most difficult and pain-filled packaging. I watched as my dad became more dependent upon me. We became more dependent on our Lord; our faith was being tested and strengthened.

> Depend on the Lord, trust him, and he
> will take care of you. (Psalm 37:5 NCV)

Have there been times in your life when life's blessings have been wrapped in tragedy? I believe that when we seek the Lord during times of challenge and deep hurt, God will truly do something amazing. It may not look like the package you wanted, but trusting God with the package will always promote blessing and favor. The world will try to make you question why God would allow this pain but believe me when I tell you—stay strong and faithful even in tragedy. God gave Job double for his troubles and tragedies, and what won't God do for you? That is right—God will do for you! So again, stay strong and faithful for God has you.

So, at this point you may be thinking about how discouraged you have been, unmotivated, hurt, or you may know someone who is going through a challenging time. What would it take for you to trust that God has you even during the storm, that He has your friend or family member in the midst of a devastating diagnosis? Honestly, it can seem overwhelming, and you may not have ever been introduced to the love of God the Father. But I am here to tell you that when you are facing a mountain, God is the Real Deal! He will meet you where you are and will join you in overcoming that mountain if you allow Him.

CHAPTER 3

THE FEATHERS

On one day when my father could still get up, he went into the bathroom. He spent a good amount of time in the restroom, pondering his slow decline and wondering what would be next. Upon checking on him, I heard him speaking as if he were talking to someone. I asked him if he was okay and he stated, "Kelly, I can't get the feathers out of my way. Honey, they won't move their wings." I opened the door and did not see anything; however, I knew he did. A cool breeze swept by.

> He will cover you with his feathers. He will shelter you with his wings. His faithful promises are your armor and protection. (Psalm 91:4 NLT)

Since that day, I have a vivid understanding that angels never leave our sides. Even after my dad departed this earth, God still saw it fit to remind me periodically that He sends his angels to watch over and protect us.

I proceeded to assist my father up and out of the bathroom. He got back to his bed, now situated in the den. He shared with me again that he just could not get to the top of the mountain, and he was frustrated that he could not reach the top. It was evidently a journey that he had to make.

Once again, I reflected on the mountain and now the feathers. What did all this mean?

The answers at this time were very new to me because I was not knowledgeable about specifics in the Bible and had never done extensive research on biblical wisdom. Discussions with my parents focused on the measures of comfort sent from God. God utilizes moments of stress and helplessness to point us to His unending love and mercy. During this journey He continually reveals that we are present for His glory and for His purpose. During my father's decline the Holy Spirit's presence comforted us and represented yet another example of the Father's love for us.

> God utilizes moments of stress and helplessness to point us to His unending love and mercy.

I was convinced that the feathers and wings were angels. Yet the psalmist writes about God's wings: "Have mercy on me, my God, have mercy on me, for in you I take refuge. I will take refuge in the shadow of your wings until the disaster has passed" (Psa. 57:1). Wow, David talks about God's wings being a refuge.

He will cover you with his feathers.
He will shelter you with his wings. His
faithful promises are your armor and
protection. (Psalm 91:4 NLT)

Honestly, I do not know if it was angels or God
Himself that day but what did ease my mind and
heart was knowing God was in our midst. He took
care of my father every moment and comforted my
family. That is love! He is with us during the storm,
the disease, and the challenge. Always at our side,
whether we acknowledge it or not.

I believe to this day that God sent Dad guard-
ian angels to comfort him and prompt him forward
in his journey. The mountain, I believe, was the
journey he was on to meet with the Lord.

Dad's endurance and continued perseverance
through this two-month process were inspiring,
and his lack of concern about the physicality of his
journey encouraged me to increase my own faith
and determination. He did not seem to sweat over
his need for assistance, and this was a man who
consistently helped and did for others. I believe
that watching him deteriorate was more painful for
my mother and me. My brother, being far away in
the army, could not see what we were seeing, and
this was difficult for him also. We were so used to
Dad, our God-given protector, provider, husband,
and father, masterfully completing tasks. Witness-

ing him in this physical state was heart-wrenching. Many of our family and friends came by to visit, bless us with comfort food, and their company. As they came, we felt encouraged and many times we shared the miraculous stories that were becoming a part of our every day.

One day my dear friend Tina came by to stay with my mother and father while I took my two-year-old son grocery shopping, desiring to spend some quality time out with him. Connor was exactly two years old and had a sweet relationship with his grandparents. It was approximately two years and four months since I had cried out to the Lord to spare my father's life for enough time to have an influence on Connor. Oh, what God will not do for us when we cry out to Him. I thanked God for giving us my son and this time. Connor and I discussed the sweet fun memories of his amazing Grampy as we started our grocery trip.

We went into the Langley Air Force Base grocery store and began walking down the aisles to pick up some items we needed. Connor was sitting in the shopping cart discussing all the items he saw at the store. As we neared the end of our grocery shopping, he became noticeably quiet and vomited all over himself and the floor. He looked as if he were in a daze. I quickly paid for the groceries and took him out to the car. He was still in a daze as if half asleep. He told me that he was with Grampy and that he was trying to stop him from going up the mountain. He said that his Grampy told him to go back.

At about the same time, I received a call from Tina. She sounded concerned and said that my father had awakened and was agitated. He said that Connor would not get out of his way—that Connor would not let him go up the mountain. As I listened and looked at my son, I realized that this could not be explained naturally, and neither could it to be a coincidence. It was another God moment. Connor did not want his Grampy to leave. I held back the tears and explained to Connor that if it should happen again, he needed to just encourage Grampy to climb that mountain. I told him that Grampy might need his help climbing this mountain and that the best way to do that was to encourage him that he could do it!

After I got Connor home with my mom and was alone, I cried. I prayed and then I cried some more. Grandfather and grandson had a strong connection and it hit me that this is what I had prayed earlier, that my dad would have an impact on my son. Connor loved his Grampy dearly and enjoyed all the occasions we had together even till my dad's last breath. He did not spend enormous amounts of time with him once my dad was bedridden, but Connor was able to see him and share moments. I can remember Connor's favorite stuffed tiger that he put beside his grandfather. He wanted him to know even if he was not there with Grampy his tiger was and all he had to do was hold it. This still brings tears to my eyes that this two-year-old could vocalize such sweetness and understanding.

Not long after my mother died, a year after my dad, Connor had a dream and was laughing while he slept in our bed. He was laughing with that sweet belly laugh that children enjoy while still asleep. Jim and I both woke up and laughed with him. It was a sweet time. The next morning, I asked Connor if he had a dream. Connor's response was, "Mom, Grammy and Grampy were telling me jokes last night." He spoke so solidly about this, as if it were more than a dream, a reality! Again, every hair on my body stood alert and I smiled, thanking God again for this joy-filled moment. My hope is that Grampy still visits Connor in his dreams, to encourage him in his walk of faith and reinforce that God is calling on his life as a young man and leader for God's kingdom in this world.

As my father deteriorated, he did not think of his own needs. He had a love so strong for my mother that all he could think of was how to take care of her. These feathers from God had come to his aid and flanked him on either side. They were there to remind my dad that even if we are not in control or when we feel we are unable, God is surely able to do beyond what we can think or fathom (see Ephesians 3:20).

Some of our angels are winged and some I believe come in the form of the Holy Spirit working through the body of Christ, the Church—God's children.

One of those people was Mr. Adams. He worked with my dad at Newport News Shipbuilding as a guard and they were buds. Many days Mr. Adams would come by to sit with my father and visit. He prayed with my dad, joked with my dad, shared common stories about "the good ole days," and talked about many things during his visits. One thing that was obvious about Mr. Adams and his wife was that they loved the Lord Jesus. They were super sweet and such a blessing to our family. To this day my son still has a little black Bible that Mr. Adams gave him. He loved the Lord and shared God's Word with anyone who would listen. I praise God for Mr. Adam's friendship and visits with my father. You can never have enough faithful Jesus-loving friends!!

Isn't it ironic that we live our lives thinking we grasp who God is and what is possible, but personal sorrow can sometimes be the catalyst to help us realize how small we have made God?

Recently I watched the movie *The Shack*. Poppa (God the Father) relates to the main character, Mac, that when all we see is our pain, we cannot see

God. God is so much grander, so much more than we can even imagine. Our limited capacity to know who and what He has done for us can sometimes fade when we are faced with the eventualities of life.

God wants us to have everlasting life with Him and whether we have spent a lifetime acknowledging His most precious Son, Jesus, or come to know Jesus at death's door, God is always patiently waiting on us and desires us to call to Him. Psalm 23:6 (NLT) says, "Surely your goodness and unfailing love will pursue me all the days of my life, and I will live in the house of the Lord forever." Sweet promises in God's Word comfort us and lead us down the less traveled road of peace and strength.

God pursues us! Wow, what an amazing thought! That when we totally mess things up, when we sin big, when we choose death, God still prods us to choose life, to choose Jesus, to live in love.

Are there times when you do not know where to turn? Have you dug yourself into a pit that you are unable to see your way out of? Are you climbing a mountain that has shown up in your life? God knows you; He knows every hair you have on your head and knows your innermost thoughts. When you say, "The Lord is my refuge, my dwelling place," He will command His angels over you and not allow harm to overtake you (see Psalm 91:9–11).

That is the Real Deal, and we have the choice to believe it, or not.

Personally, I believe God's angels protect and lovingly look out for God's children. It is only when I claim God is my refuge and know the sacrifice He has made for me that I am His child. Yes, we are created in His image, but to be heirs to eternal life, we have been given the right to choose. God does not force us; He desires us to choose life, to choose Him.

Just as a note to you, dear reader, these signs, dreams, and visions shared are not the end or what I abide in. God allowed me these instances to direct my steps to Him and His Word in the Bible. My hope is that you too will see God working in your life and in your situations and be led as I have been to the Real Deal in His Word, the Bible.

Living our lives from pleasure to pleasure is only gratifying for the present and leads to emptiness and eventually destruction. When we live from faith to faith, we see God's glory shine through the darkness, and His light fills up the empty places that only God can fill. I pray you have angels surround you as you continue to read and draw near to the Way, the Truth, and the Life—Jesus Christ.

CHAPTER 4

FROM TWO TO FOUR AND FOUR TO TWO

My father shared a confusing statement with me in 2003 as he was nearing death. The words he shared would have an eternal impact on how I lived my life. Every day since these words were spoken, I have attempted to understand what he was trying to tell me. If you will open your heart, you may understand what I believe God was bringing into focus and desiring to make clear to us.

As I proceed to disclose this information I do so cautiously, and only with acknowledgment that God is big, His ways are good, and it is His message that is the Real Deal.

One afternoon during my father's journey up the mountain, he shared something he did not want me to forget. He was extremely specific so that I would not forget, and I listened carefully. He stated that he had something to share, and I obliged by giving him my attention. My dad went on to say these words:

"From two to four and four to two, they can switch 'em."

My response was, "I don't understand, Dad."

He repeated, "From two to four and four to two."

I again responded with, "I still don't understand what you mean, Dad."

At that he lovingly stated, "Kelly, you are very smart—you will get it; don't worry, you will understand one day." Well, it is twenty years later, and I am much closer to a full understanding of this statement but always open to God's continual work in me through His Word.

One evening, after my father had passed, I sat out on my back patio with my husband, Jim, and our friend, Joel. They listened as I shared this information with them, and we discussed what my dad might have meant. I was given the comfort that God would reveal it to me in time.

During our conversation, their voices faded out and my eyes focused on the clearly burning light bulb in the sconce on our deck. My eyes fixed on the glow that surrounded the bulb. The glow shone golden, and the light spread outside the perimeter of the bulb's glass. As that bulb burned with a glow that spilled out beyond the walls containing it, I suddenly felt in my spirit that God was going to work on supplying my every need and answering the questions that remained. I thanked God and would remember His promise that He would reveal all things in time.

> But my God shall supply all your need according to his riches in glory by Christ Jesus. (Philippians 4:19 KJV)

> And now at just the right time he has revealed this message, which we announce to everyone. It is by the command of God our Savior that I have been entrusted with this work for him. (Titus 1:3)

Over a period of many years, I would share my dad's statement about "two to four and four to two" with others that I thought might be able to help me discern the meaning. Time after time after discussing this with others, I would leave still searching. There was something profound about those words; I knew that one day it would all make sense. Many times, I struggled and found myself grasping at straws to find the answer; patience was and still is an area I need refinement in. But each time my impatience resurfaced, I chose to trust God and learn to press into His Word, the Bible.

> Trust in the Lord with all your heart and lean not on your own understanding. (Proverbs 3:5)

I remember sharing this "two to four and four to two" statement with some strong believers, figuring that surely they would know what these words meant. They were rooted in the Bible and would be considered elders in many churches. After sharing, I was no closer to an answer. In fact, their response was not as gratifying as I had hoped it would be. Once again, I had to rely only on God's promise. God's ways are not our ways.

> "For my thoughts are not your thoughts, neither are your ways my ways," declares the Lord. "As the heavens are higher than the earth, so are my ways higher than your ways and my thoughts than your thoughts." (Isaiah 55:8–9)

I think that so many times we turn to other people and seek their thoughts on a particular topic or subject. Yet God wants us to come to Him first and continually. He may not reveal answers immediately, but God will reveal truth in His timing, and it will always line up with His Word, the Bible. Prayer and God's Word should be our primary go-to, not other people or internet searches.

Now, let me say I do believe that God gave us one another to grow with, and be in relationship with, but our main source of wisdom and knowledge should come from God through the Bible, His infallible Word, and the workings of His Holy Spirit.

That way when we need assistance from those dear to us, we will know if it's in agreement with the Word of God. I have dear friends that are believers and unbelievers. When I have a biblical question, I go to the Bible and pray. If I cannot figure it out, I ask a friend who knows God's Word. I am in the Word daily so that I can follow the standard that has been given to us. When I have any question, I can go to friends whether they are believers or not or utilize Google as a resource. If it lines up with the standard that leads my life, it helps. If not, I'm still appreciative because I have friends I trust and love and tools like the internet that are at my disposal. Yet not everything that looks good or sounds good is right. Not even if things agree with how we feel or think. It is a dangerous trap to think that our feelings or thoughts or ideas are facts or truth. They are the way you think and feel and are your beliefs in who you are, not always factual or truthful.

As I think about this, I can assuredly promise you that if you go to the Lord, seek His presence, and turn to His Word in Scripture, He will reveal the truth. His Word is Truth! The Holy Spirit gives us a magnifying glass to the importance of His Word, which I like to refer to as "Holy Spirit highlighter." The light bulb turns on, so to speak. It is God and His answers that will sustain us, not our own reasoning. We are limited; He is limitless!

So, I continued to search for answers and took time to read the Bible. Doors opened for me to attend Bible studies and I consistently prayed for answers. I was so hungry for more answers from God. I had to remember to be patient, and as I previously said this is not my nature at all. Many times, during my quest for answers I felt like a child trying to force puzzle pieces into the wrong spaces. At times, truthfully, I would get so frustrated, and the one thing that helped me through was prayer. I continually rested on God's promises and acknowledged that in time the answers would be revealed.

God reveals Himself in His timing, not ours. He never goes back on His Word and always follows through on His promises. He will reveal Himself to you if you search and desire Him with your whole heart. It is not easy, but you need to completely let go and trust that God has you.

Have you ever taken swimming lessons? Do you remember when you learned to do the back float? If you do not swim, watch someone who is learning the back float for the first time. As you lie back in the water and almost begin to float, you suddenly begin flailing your arms due to fear and an uneasy feeling, unsure that you can stay afloat. The fact is that you will eventually float, but it takes time, and you must continue to try. After a few attempts you begin to realize that the water will hold you up. Well, coming to have faith and trust in Jesus

Christ is a lot like doing the back float for the first time. At first, you are fearful; you cannot see God, and you are not sure of the meaning of the Bible's words. Then you might pray that God would reveal Himself and that you desire a relationship with Him through His Son, Jesus. It is during this time that God's movements and supports begin to be more evident, because He truly desires a relationship with you and wants you to know Him. When you begin to understand the Bible and that it is God's infallible Word, you will have learned the back float. Now, in a pool with no ripples a back float is quite easy, but in the ocean, with its waves, it gets harder, but you can still do it.

Our lives after we accept Jesus are not always going to be easy or trouble-free, but trusting God during those troubled times will bring you to a deeper understanding. It is only through testing that our strength and faith will grow. Much like trusting the water's buoyant force in doing a back float, we must trust that God will uphold us. Our faith grows as we trust in the way, the truth, and the life, Jesus Christ (see John 14:6).

So let go and let God; He will take you higher than you have ever been. He will lift you up. Isaiah 40:31 reminds us that "they who wait for the LORD shall renew their strength; they shall mount up with wings like eagles; they shall run and not be weary; they shall walk and not faint" (ESV). Another Bible translation says hope in the Lord.

I choose to wait, to hope. As I have gotten better at my back float, I realize that my body becomes more buoyant as I take in air. When I exhale, my body becomes less buoyant. In this same way, the more I take in of God's Word and trust in Him, the better and stronger I grow. It is those times I put God on the back burner and just exhale that I fall into old destructive patterns of living.

Every so often, as the years passed, God would remind me of the words my father shared, and I would ponder them and continue to wait on the Lord, fully expecting that I would be given understanding one day.

On August 23, 2011, I received an answer. I just started a new job as a kindergarten teacher, at a new school. I was setting up my classroom in preparation for the big first day of kindergarten and suddenly there was a slight shaking of the building and a loud boom. I inquired as to what the movement was, and a coworker presumed it was someone working on the building or up on the roof. I went back to organizing my new room, cleaning, and setting it up.

Later that same day as I drove home from work, I was stopped in traffic on the bridge. My phone dinged as I was at a full stop and the daily Scripture verse popped up on my Bible app: "Therefore keep watch, because you do not know on what day your Lord will come" (Matt. 24:42). Little did I realize the implications this verse had on this day.

That same evening, I found out that the rumble I felt and boom I heard while setting up my classroom was an earthquake here in Virginia! I have lived here in Hampton Roads for most of my life and never once have we had an earthquake. It was no coincidence that on the same day a verse foreshadowing the second coming of Jesus popped up on my phone.

Now let us look closer at that Scripture verse: Matthew 24:42. The digits 2, 4, 4, 2 stood out to me. Those numbers sent shivers straight through me as I remembered my father's words, "two to four and four to two." I still get Holy Spirit tingles when I think about this moment. It feels like chills, although these goose bumps are welcome. An earthquake and Jesus's own words in the Book of Matthew now revealed the answer I had been seeking for so many years. I was astonished. After this day I found it more difficult to sit back; I had to move forward in Christ and share salvation with all who would listen. Stay alert, awake, keep watch, and don't grow numb or callous to all that is going on. The Lord will come again and when He returns, we need to be aware and ready for His coming!

This verse in Matthew commands us to "stay awake" and to "keep watch." No one knows the time

Jesus will come again but we are to be prepared for that time. How do we prepare? When we prepare for weddings, hurricanes, and other big events, we have supplies ready for the occasion. In preparing for the second coming of Jesus, we must stay close to God in prayer, immerse ourselves in His Word, the Bible, and stay plugged into the church, the body of Christ made up of believers. To be alert and aware, we need to know what we are looking at and what we are alert for. I cannot take an exam and do well if I have merely looked at the material and not really studied it. It is funny how we sometimes look at our faith as being a one-way download from God, when truly it is a two-way relationship, one that gives us everything we need to be ready for our eternal destiny. The Word of God is living and active and we grow continually by staying in it. We will have knowledge and increase in love for God, others, and ourselves if we will trust God and stay in His Word.

> Living a life for Christ doesn't mean that I am perfect or better than anyone. It is acknowledging that Christ is perfect, and I am God's child and set apart and different, not better!

Living a life for Christ doesn't mean that I am perfect or better than anyone. It is acknowledging that Christ is perfect, and I am God's child and set apart and different, not better! His sacrifice on the cross wipes away all my imperfections. His righteousness gives me eternal life. God sees those who know and trust through the sacrifice of His Son, Jesus Christ. Just as we prepare and are alert for weather events and celebrations, we are to live life preparing to meet Jesus again through authentically living our lives God's way.

Living in Christ also means that I know I have a guide with me, the Holy Spirit. Jesus specifically told believers that "the helper," the Holy Spirit, would come to comfort, protect, and guide us. So much love from the Father. And yet, amazingly, we get to choose whether to accept this precious gift or not. It is not a forced relationship, and God is faithful and patient. Nothing can ever separate us from His love, but we must make the choice to follow Him, and honestly, it is a daily choice. Sometimes it is a "moment-by-moment" choice and through each "yes" to God our endurance builds and our life in Christ matures.

Our days are numbered, whether by Christ's second coming or by the day or night we will leave this earth. I have lost many people in my life who have written me off because of my zeal and passion for the Lord. I make no apologies; I have "crazy faith," but it is this faith that has set me free. It is not with condemnation that I appeal to friends and strangers or you; it is with love. Oh, how much

God genuinely loves you and wants you to come to Him. It is with a heavy heart that some have not heeded the very same warning that came from Matthew. BE ALERT, STAY AWAKE! COME AND FOLLOW JESUS CHRIST.

Two Scriptures pop out to me as I have been writing this chapter:

> I eagerly expect and hope that I will in no way be ashamed but will have sufficient courage so that now as always Christ will be exalted in my body, whether by life or by death. For to me, to live is Christ and to die is gain. If I am to go on living in the body, this will mean fruitful labor for me. Yet what shall I choose? I do not know! I am torn between the two: I desire to depart and be with Christ, which is better by far; but it is more necessary for you that I remain in the body.
>
> Convinced of this, I know that I will remain, and I will continue with all of you for your progress and joy in the faith, so that through my being with you again your boasting in Christ Jesus will abound on account of me. (Philippians 1:20–27)

> I have been crucified with Christ and I
> no longer live, but Christ lives in me. The
> life I now live in the body, I live by faith
> in the Son of God, who loved me and
> gave himself for me. I do not set aside
> the grace of God, for if righteousness
> could be gained through the law, Christ
> died for nothing! (Galatians 2:20–21)

Are there questions in your life that you are growing impatient to have answered? Have you given
up on your dreams and desires? Are you afraid to
go "all in" for Jesus? My advice to you is to never
give up and never fear! It took me over twenty years
to realize what was important and what was real.
I imagine for many people it takes less time and
for some, more, but however long it takes you, do
not give up! God never gives up on you! There may
be many things you do not understand and some
things you are definite about—take them all to the
Lord. He will assist you in purging lies and keeping
hold of the truths. God loves us, no matter what we
have done, no matter what we have believed. He is
forever by our side waiting for us, for that moment
when we realize how very much He loves us and
is overjoyed when we accept Jesus into our hearts.

> For God so loved the world, that He
> gave His only begotten Son, that
> whoever believes in Him should not

perish but have everlasting life. (John 3:16 NKJV)

That verse says it all: God loved us (loves us) so much that He sent His Son, Jesus Christ, to live a life not as a king but as a human being. Jesus took on all our sins, died on the cross, and was resurrected so that we would be in relationship with God and would one day join Jesus in heaven. God is so good, His Son is the Real Deal, and history proves He existed, proves He died, proves He came back, and proves many of the Bible's tenets.

Wow! Do not let ignorance or stubbornness keep you from the promises God has for you. Oh, how sweet it is to live a life in Christ, better than any of the ways I chose to live prior to my submitting everything to Christ. I pray you will accept Jesus as your Lord and Savior. Not because it's in style or because someone is telling you to, but because you have chosen! All must choose for themselves. It is a gift you can either receive and open or push away, but no matter what, Jesus's sacrifice was for us! It is the Real Deal!

CHAPTER 5

"WHY ARE YOU DOING THIS?"

> You have searched me, LORD, and you know me. (Psalm 139:1)
>
> Would not God have discovered it since he knows the secrets of the heart? (Psalm 44:21)
>
> But the LORD said to Samuel, "Do not look at his appearance or at the height of his stature, because I have rejected him; for God sees not as a man sees, for man looks at the outward appearance, but the LORD looks at the heart." (1 Samuel 16:7 NASB)

Many times, our intentions, good or bad, honorable, or dishonorable, go undetected.... Yet God knows our intentions; He knows our hearts. As we begin our journey with the Lord, we have a desire for God to set our hearts right, to check the intentions of our hearts.

This will be the most sensitive, personal, and transparent revelation of all that is in this book. It is my hope that it will help you to see how much Father God loves you and desires you to forgive yourself and others as He has forgiven you. When we sin, it is important that we acknowledge that we have fallen short by sin and that we need Jesus Christ our Savior. Repent the sin, ask to be forgiven, and accept God's forgiveness through His Son, Jesus Christ. Jesus took all our sin on the cross!

Sin and forgiveness were things that I did not fully comprehend, and they became distorted through my early church experience. I thought that the priest was my mediator to God for my sin. In the old Jewish faith this would have been true. In the Old Testament, the priest would take your offering to the altar once a year to absolve you of sin. In the church I grew up in we would have to go to confession frequently to tell our sins and were then given absolution by a priest. We would have to make a penance, something we needed to pray or do, to be fully absolved. I can tell you now, from reading God's Word, that the sacrifice Jesus made for us absolves us from all sin. Scripture says to "confess your sins to one another, and pray for one another so that you may be healed" (Jas. 5:16 NASB).

When I understood this, it was something that freed me from the baggage of sin. There was no saving up my sins to tell a priest. When I sin, I go straight to the cross of Christ and ask for forgiveness. I ask for assistance from the Holy Spirit not to sin again. The most freeing thing I ever did was realize what God's Son, Jesus Christ, did for me; Jesus's death and resurrection took my sin and yours and gave us new life. That is why it is so important to recognize and acknowledge Jesus as your Lord and Savior. The sacrifice of Jesus gives us His righteousness to be in right relationship with God. People can pray for us; only Jesus can save and set us free. There is nothing we can do to earn it or lose it once we have committed our lives to salvation through Jesus Christ.

Our Father's love is unlike any other love we can know. He showed His love by sending His Son, Jesus, to die for us. God desires to have a personal relationship with us through His Son. He knew we were not strong enough or pure enough to pull ourselves out of the pit of sin. No matter what we do it will never be enough to cover the multitude of sins. We can never be good enough, and that's why God sent His only Son, Jesus, to overcome the pit of hell. Jesus alone gives us hope in heaven. We are loved and we matter to God. Whether your earthly father loved you is not what matters. What matters is that Your Father, Abba, wants you to know peace, joy, hope, and love in relationship with Him. He loves us all and He gave us all the ultimate sign of love, His Son, Jesus Christ.

As the days passed, my father and I shared many conversations. Sweet quality time in conversation during his last breaths on this earth. He shared his love to the end. He showed his love to the end. He would have sacrificed all just to know that his family, especially my mother, was okay. My father loved us.

It was getting near the end of my dad's journey. He woke up from napping and inquired, "Kelly, why are you here? Why are you doing what you are doing?" I didn't fully understand what my dad was asking or why.

He asked again, "Why are you doing this?" He seemed insistent with this question. I responded, "Because I love you, Daddy." Surely, he must know!

My dad was not asking me because he wanted to know for himself. He wanted me to know what my motive was. He knew I loved him, but he tested my motives. God prompts us to be honest in our motives, to have a right heart.

Oh, how I loved my dad and never wanted to say goodbye. When tears flowed and I asked what more I could do, he responded in the most loving way, "You are doing a good job, honey. I love you." Not only did my father know that I needed reassurance and affirmation due to my human frailty, but God knows what we need. God speaks to us through His Word and He speaks to us through others, through nature, and through signs and wonders. When we begin a relationship with Jesus, we realize that He will reach us where we are, no matter where. As we seek more of God, we begin to see God in everything. We start to see the world through the frame that He created us to see it in. God lifted the veil through Christ Jesus and as we grow in our relationship with Him the veil over our heart is lifted as God shares knowledge with us.

For many years I thought back to the time my father had questioned me so earnestly about my intentions: "Why are you doing this?" Throughout my life he had never questioned me this way. He always believed in me, no matter how many times I disappointed him. He always loved me unconditionally! His love was unfailing, a good example of our Father's love. As I mentioned before, my dad was incredibly loving, and we were extremely close. He always knew what to say and how to speak to me.

God loves us more than that! Being in God's Word shows me repeatedly about having a pure heart and right motives. The apostle Paul tells us anything outside of truth in our heart will be uncovered. Many times, when I was in doubt as a young child, thinking sad or fearful things, my dad would reassure me to think beautiful, good, pure things. As I got older this reassurance would come back to me.

> Finally, brothers and sisters, whatever is true, whatever is noble, whatever is right, whatever is pure, whatever is lovely, whatever is admirable—if anything is excellent or praiseworthy—think about such things. (Philippians 4:8)

After my father died, I became even more interested in God's Word. I realized that my dad from the beginning of my life had poured into me one of the most amazing biblical foundations. God led me to what my dad taught me. Philippians 4:8 was becoming a reality in my life! "Think on things that are good, pure, lovely, admirable, excellent, or praiseworthy." This is God's desire for all.

I always found it interesting when people would share the Scriptures they memorized in their youth or their family's input of Scripture and quotes from the Bible. Growing up I knew our family loved God, the Lord Jesus, and the Holy Spirit, but we didn't memorize Scripture. Although memorizing is also wonderful, and I do it now, Scripture should be written in our hearts and expressed in our words and actions. It is the foundational food that we eat. God's Word sustains us!

When I was scared or afraid, my dad would sit with me and ask me to think about good things.

Then, as he was on his journey, soon to be home with our Lord and Savior Jesus, he asked me, "Why?" Why? Why did he ask this so intensely as he neared death? All I could think of was how he had loved me when I could not love myself, when I felt judged, when I felt alone, when I felt ugly, when I could not find the answers—he loved me! "I am doing what I am doing because you first loved me!" What a correlation to the Bible. When we realize how much God loves us, our decisions and actions begin to come from a place of overwhelming love because God first loved us by giving His only Son, Jesus.

God tells us in the New Testament what love is: "To lay down one's life for another." Whether that be stepping in front of a bullet or putting your own needs to the side to put others first, love takes the "I" or "me" out of life and brings HIM to the forefront. So even when we don't think we can love anymore, HE will, and HE does. Wow, Dad, I pray Jesus is sharing with you right now how much I love you and appreciate all you instilled in me. I love you because you first loved me.

Still, the question, "Why are you doing this?" stayed with me years after my father's death.

Many times, we may not think of our intentions as being selfish. God looks at our motives; He desires us to be pure in our hearts. When my father asked me, "Why are you doing this?" I immediately answered, "Because I love you." But being asked this by my father, thinking he knew why, made me search my heart. It made me reflect on all that I had done and what I was doing in the present. What was my focus? Who is my focus?

For years, people search for meaning, for the definition of love, for their identity, all the while never realizing that it comes from one place. It is that love of God that sets us free, and until we know that love, we spend our time running around aimlessly from pleasure to pleasure, pain to pain, when all along God desires us to live faith to faith. Living in faith results in blessing, abundant blessing. It is not the blessing that the world defines, but the blessing that our Father in heaven defines, and it is so beyond my capacity to describe here. His blessing is much more vast, exclusive, and amazing. It makes what has been fractured whole. It takes out the mess and, in its place, becomes the shine, the sparkle, and the light of Christ. God's blessing makes a garden in place of the grave, makes beauty from ashes, and gives a message to the mess.

> God's blessing makes a garden in place of the grave, makes beauty from ashes, and gives a message to the mess.

I understand how people spend their lives living from pleasure to pleasure and pain to pain over accepting the love, freedom, and peace of Jesus Christ. I did this for many years. Even then, God loved me, and He loves you. What are you doing? How are you spending your life?

The Creator of the universe loves us so much that He sent His only Son that whoever believes in Him would not perish but have eternal life (see John 3:16).

Each of us needs to answer the question, "Why are you doing this?" What's your "why?" Is it an external gratification? Or is it internal? When we are searching and figuring out our motives, Jesus and the power of the Holy Spirit will become more real in the revelation given. Don't be afraid of this; we all have ways we deal with life and thankfully God knows and will work in you that which is holy and pure, and will work out the impurities.

In the midst of this question came another conversation in which my father woke up from a nap and began to ask me about a season of sin in my life. I was dumbfounded, not thinking that he or my mother ever knew the specifics. I questioned him and asked what he meant. He repeated the question. I stared out our back patio window, tears streaming down my face. I answered my father with, "I don't know, Daddy…. I am sorry…. I never meant to…" (live in the sinful situation in which I had lived).

Now the question he asked was quite specific, but rather than getting into the details I'll just say that it was a sinful period in my life that I was deeply ashamed of and had a large baggage of guilt, shame, and unworthiness attached to it. I made many mistakes and had wandered far from where God and my parents would have wanted me to be. I thought my parents had known absolutely nothing about what I was doing.

I told my dad to rest, quickly departed the room, grabbed the phone, and proceeded to call my Aunt Jane from outside in our garage. She was the only one I shared my struggles with during this time of my life. Tears rolling down my face, I asked my aunt if she had spoken with my parents and she said no, never about that particular area. I continued to weep and told her what had happened. She honestly didn't understand how he knew and even said that my mom and dad would have come to her if they had known.

Then, after I got off the phone with my aunt, I sat down in the dining room with my mother. She could see I was distraught and knew something was wrong and asked me if everything was okay. I told her that I needed to tell her something, explaining that I was sorry, and that I never wanted my parents to know. Sobbing, I asked her how she knew.

My mom shared that she knew nothing about this situation. She assured me this was not something they ever thought I would have been involved in. I bawled my eyes out, asked my mother for forgiveness, and she held me tightly for a few moments, telling me she loved me. Then she told me to let it go. She said that she and my dad could not be any prouder and that she had prayed that whatever I had gone through, God would see me through. Wow!!

Well, God saw me through! He allowed me to make choices, good and bad; that's free will. He also allowed me to carry the burden of these sins even after I had confessed to a priest. God doesn't desire us to carry the burden of our sin or unforgiveness. Don't we often do just that, carry our sins even after we are repentant? Do we carry others' sins in judgment, holding them accountable to expectations? God's forgiveness is real, and it covers a multitude of sins, all sin. All the world's sins are what kept Jesus on the cross. God loved us that much! Yet in order to truly forgive, you must let go and let God. Seriously, He is the only one who can release you and give you lasting peace. Harboring unforgiveness is like receiving a gift but refusing to open it. Forgiveness comes when we fully recognize what Jesus has done for us and then leave that sin, shame, guilt, and unworthiness at the foot of the cross at Jesus's feet.

I believe this very situation was another God appointment, His working through my father to release me of the sin that I clung to for fear that it was too bad to be truly forgiven. A "mortal" sin that I had been taught in private school could send me straight to hell. Now, at that time I did not understand that all sin is the same in God's eyes. Some sin is more detrimental to us because of what it causes in our lives and to our mortal bodies, but God looks at stealing, lying, adultery, pride, and murder, as the same. But for me, I looked at my sin as being the absolute worst. I guess because it was not something I ever thought I would do. I can tell you now that I turn from sin and look to the Sin Forgiver! Just saying the name of Jesus is more powerful than the clutches of sin and I choose to walk with God and accept His gift of forgiveness!

> Instead of looking through a lens of loss, I look through the victory that we all have through Jesus.

Instead of looking through a lens of loss, I look through the victory that we all have through Jesus. What lens are you looking through? Has what society said is okay or not okay blinded you to the truth of what God says? Honestly, if you are stuck in a pit of sin, look to our Savior, Jesus, and He will free you from sin's bondage.

I can remember the freedom I had after truly letting go of the guilt of sin committed, and the shame I connected to it. The invisible load I was carrying dropped off and I did not pick it back up. God did not create us to wallow or walk in guilt and shame. He sent Jesus to free us of that imprisonment and work out our salvation by being a vessel for the Holy Spirit. It is that simple and yet we complicate it by not forgiving ourselves. Do not hold yourself or anyone else hostage by holding onto sins. Our God sent His Son, Jesus, to free us from these entanglements and far be it from us to refuse His gift of redemption through Christ Jesus.

Millions of people play the lottery, looking for the opportunity to win and live an abundant life. It often amazes me how many people run and grow weary in the world's definition of abundance. Why, when we can run and never grow weary?

> But those who hope in the LORD will renew their strength. They will soar on wings like eagles; they will run and not grow weary; they will walk and not be faint. (Isaiah 40:31)

We run to what is free in this world but refuse to accept the free gift of salvation. It takes one choice, one moment, to begin your life in love. No matter what you've done or what's been done to you, you have the choice to accept, and believe truth. Once you believe, the work begins and it is amazing what your Father in heaven does. He will renew your strength and fill you with the Holy Spirit. This choice and acceptance make us a new creation; we are transformed.

> Do not conform to the pattern of this world but be transformed by the renewing of your mind. Then you will be able to test and approve what God's will is—his good, pleasing, and perfect will. (Romans 12:2)

To receive God's gift of love and forgiveness you need only to choose Jesus, and then be open to the new creation that you were meant to be! God will not force us, and the enemy is doing everything he can to keep us from having the everlasting life that God promises. While you are reading, I am praying that you accept Jesus as your Savior, get into a Bible-based Christian church, and allow the Holy Spirit to guide you on the path to righteousness. A righteousness that was bought with a high price, the price of Jesus dying on the cross. I pray that salvation will be yours.

God loves you so much.

CHAPTER 6

FILLING THE VOID

As I have been writing this book each chapter reminds me of the insight that our Father God has given me through the power of the Holy Spirit and the Word. Obstacles and challenges that need to be overcome are difficult to face, let alone overcome, yet through Christ all things are possible (see Philippians 4:13).

I have known the Lord Jesus all my life. At a young age a sense of Him was poured into me through the Catholic faith. I treasure worshipful reverence that the Catholic Church instilled in me. Where I floundered was establishing and maintaining a personal relationship with the Lord and staying close to Him through my young adult years.

Through the years I would go to confession with a heart aching to be forgiven, but even with the act of contrition and the penance given I still felt judged, sin-filled, and at times dirty and shameful. The sad thing is that it didn't matter how many times I went to confession, I never fully felt free from sin, nor was I able to let others be freed when they offended me. On the outside I was a "good girl" because I followed all the rules that I thought would free me. On the inside I was piling up an avalanche that would soon fall on my world. I truly had no understanding of the full power of the Holy Spirit and His purpose in my life.

When I went off to college, I did not nourish my relationship with Christ, yet God was present as He is in all our lives. Many times, I would run to Him and He would gently lead me and at times He spoke to my heart. Sometimes I ran away; I would not be consistent with God until much later.

During those years I often looked to others to fill the voids and holes that were never filled. I wanted people to answer the questions that God wanted to answer. I desired the affirmation and love that God so freely gave, yet I was not open to receive. I wanted people to nurse the wounds that God so desired to heal. Little did I understand that the purpose of Jesus coming, dying on the cross, and resurrecting was to meet the very needs that I was desperately searching to fulfill. Whether through people or habits, I wanted to feel content, fulfilled, identified, and whole.

I know I unintentionally hurt people in this search for affirmation and love. Not the least of those hurt were my parents. Although they were so proud of my accomplishments in college, when I came home my accomplishments would fade to the background when I would not honor God with my life choices. My parents loved me through those times. Many friends did too, but even the love of parents and friends couldn't lift the weight of guilt I carried over the wreckage I was making of my life.

Like many of us, I made choices based on feelings and desires rather than on seeking the best that God wanted for me and on checking with Him first. If it felt good and was not outside of the parameters I was setting, it was okay. I could love God and have a relationship with Him but live life by my terms without any regard to what He desired for my life. Wow, was I far out in the world, and its influence on me was numbing me to God's voice. I chose entertainment, friends, and situations that did not honor God, but thankfully God continued to love me.

God continues to love all of us! Today I tend to think this love is why Jesus stayed on the cross—for those challenging cases, like me, who continually torture themselves by not recognizing or accepting the love, peace, hope, and endless joy that Jesus has for all. Jesus Christ is the healing prescription that many neglect to fill. Why? Distractions, love for other things, and so forth. I chose unhealthy ways to deal with relationships. When I was hurt, I would dull the pain with nicotine or alcohol. I have since understood that spiritually and emotionally unhealthy people engage in unhealthy relationships, and until we deal with our unhealthy state, we will continue to hurt those we desire to love. Many times, I depended on others to define my purpose and I still need to be careful that I do not fall into that unhealthy trap.

People search for purpose and attempt to fill voids ever present in our beings with things that do not and will not satisfy or sustain us. Hurt people hurt people. Oh, the time we waste fumbling for answers rather than consulting with the One who knows!

When a relationship in the unhealthy season of my life ended, I had even bigger holes and hurt than before. And that is what happens to so many who live outside the will of God. We live according to our desires and fill ourselves with stuff, only to be more wounded than when we started. I felt filthy inside, and I was angry. I wanted to tarnish who I was because I was a good girl. Yet, inside, invisible to others, this good girl's wounds ran deep.

Well, I certainly tried to heal the wounds that ran deep with alcohol and drugs during this time of my life. Many times, I should have been dead and somehow was not. Honestly, I was just about done. To this day I thank God for strengthening me and saving me from what felt like a bottomless pit.

I have to say that I thought I was okay, comparing myself to others and feeling not as bad as her or him. On the inside I was hurting, feeling ashamed, like constantly treading water and feeling close to drowning. I paddled a lot! I ran from place to place to find the answers. I needed to hear hear "you're okay," "you are loved," "you are forgiven," "you're welcome," "you're beautiful"—anything that would make me feel whole. The devil utilized these needs to set so many traps, and because I wasn't nurturing my relationship with the Lord and filling my mind with His Word, I would fall for the traps and feel worse than ever. Any wholeness I received was temporary at best, and in the end, empty.

As the empty pit got deeper and deeper the shame and guilt did too. After an exceptionally long night I made a phone call. The recipient made an ultimatum—to leave this awful life of filling up on the wrong stuff or to be "found out" by the only two people who I knew genuinely loved me, my mom and dad. You see, I had hidden a lot from my parents during this season of my life. One person I called in desperation said, "I don't care how much your parents hate me. I will come over there and tell them face to face what you are doing. This is not who you are." My best friend also gave me an ultimatum, "If you continue this, we cannot be friends. I don't recognize you anymore." It was something of an intervention, I suppose, but these were the very things God used to kick-start my journey out of the wreckage I had created. God uses it all and nothing is wasted when it comes to His far-reaching love and how deep His love is for us.

Now this was the turning point. I did not want to disappoint my parents again. I wasn't sure how much longer their unconditional love would stretch, and I didn't want to find out. I thank God and often think of others who may be in that same trap, the ones I know and the ones I don't. I pray for each one to be rescued from the pit of their choices.

God has a way of showing up during situations and healing wounds that you did not think would ever be healed. I still had to find a way to forgive. To forgive myself mainly, but also to forgive others for the hurts that had piled up and limited my ability to live fully alive.

The choice was easy at that time, and I confessed my sins, but I never really forgave myself for making some of the choices I made. I blamed incidents, people, and history rather than just confessing that I sinned and fell short, and that I needed Jesus and forgiveness. In addition, I felt so scarred from the wrong paths that I didn't feel worthy of much. I checked myself constantly to make sure that I was making good choices. I lived in fear of making a mistake, and this is not the life God desired for me.

Needless to say, I was carrying around a large bag of guilt and shame for years before my father's cancer. My parents knew that I had been rebellious, to put it mildly, but never knew the extent. God was the only one who knew the extent of that pit. My Aunt Jane, who was my cheerleader, encourager, and guide through the toughest of times, also knew but had always promised to keep it between the two of us. She kept that promise. I believe that her love and acceptance during my worst time really was another miracle of God's redeeming love. She knew EVERYTHING and loved me despite it all. Everyone needs an Aunt Jane in their lives; I hope and pray that you have one too!

> I can do all things through him who gives me strength. (Philippians 4:13)

Forgive yourself today, leave the life that doesn't glorify God, and come to the cross with all your baggage. God made a way for me; He blasted the enemy with truth and helped me to let go of the guilt and shame from the choices I made. They no longer had a hold on me; I was no longer in bondage and could move forward after forgiving myself. From that day forward a new relationship was established. It would not come to its full potential until many years later but the relationship between Christ and me was regained, and I was ready for the Holy Spirit to move in my life. I am a witness to God's love and mercy, and He continues to mold me as the potter molds his clay (see Isaiah 64:8; Jeremiah 18; Romans 9:21).

Often, we continue to condemn ourselves. This is not pleasing to God. He wants us to seek Him and be free from the chains that bind us. We cling to the chains, afraid that we are not good enough or have sinned too much. We clothe ourselves in an attempt to cover up our sin as Adam and Eve attempted to do. God says that He will NEVER leave us or forsake us (see Hebrews 13:5). That truth does not have an "if" at the end; if we are good enough, if we work enough, if we clean ourselves up first. Jesus says that He is enough. He paid the price, and we are free because of Him. We deserve to live and love because Christ first loved us.

> God says that He will NEVER leave us or forsake us (see Hebrews 13:5). That truth does not have an "if" at the end.

The details of this life can hinder us or make us stronger. Choosing strength in Christ means surrendering the "ifs!" God already knows the finished product He has in you, so believe it, repent, forgive, and have faith!

CHAPTER 7

IN THE WAITING

For everything there is a season, a
time for every activity under heaven.
(Ecclesiastes 3:1)

God always guides His children with love, wisdom, and discipline. God's ways are always
purposeful and intentional. When God's ways seem
foreign to us, we need to look at what is going on in
our lives. Are we choosing to be near to the Lord or
are we trying to do things our way instead of God's
much better way? God gave us Jesus as the sacrifice
for sin so that we would come to know Him, to be
in relationship with Him. Then, even though bad
things happen, God makes it all work out for good
and for His glory. Oh, how God's holy words ring
true! God is willing to listen to our troubles, but do
we go to Him first? Do we surrender to Him or do
we continue to live our lives without surrendering?

Now, back to my story. My dad was meticulous
when it came to the landscaping and exterior of
our home. He made sure that the bushes were always trimmed, weeds pulled, flowers planted, leaves

raked, and lawn manicured. Upon retirement, my dad had built a pond in our backyard. Along with all the tulips and trees and bushes it was another work of art. It would be my dad's last project in glorifying God through his gardening. He would work outside in the yard from after his early morning cup of coffee until he would sit down for dinner in the evening.

When the cancer snuck back in, he had just started bringing the patio furniture out, getting all the plants potted, and performing miscellaneous other tasks out on the back patio.

That day in June, as the summer heat came through the window, my father awoke to say that the patio was in disarray and needed to be cleaned up. He said, "I cannot go yet, Kelly. Go take care of the patio. I cannot go yet." Honestly, I had no idea why he was even concerned with the patio, nor could he know that it was in disarray, because he hadn't seen the patio in over a month. In addition, I was not a horticulturalist, and my green thumb was not, and still is not, green. The view from his hospital bed in the den was quite limited so I had no idea how he could see the patio.

Again he asked me, "Kelly, please go take care of the back. I just can't leave it like this."

So, Mom and I decided that I would work on it that very day. As I began straightening and cleaning up the back patio, I realized it was a larger chore than what I believed it would be. I was partially done but still there were more things that needed to be completed. I thought to myself of the hard work my father had put into this beautiful yard and began to admire him even more for his diligence and persistence in making sure things were "in their place." Growing up I never realized the time and diligence he took at making our yard so beautiful.

The next day my dad awoke from a sleep. We laughed and joked, ate and drank, and gave thanks to God for giving us another day together. Then my dad said, "Kelly, please go finish up the patio." I looked at him and said that it was done. His response was, "No, it is not complete. Please finish it." At this point I realized my dad didn't want anything left unsettled. He mumbled some other things to do with the fact that he was working everything out with God and that there was this "deal" he had made.

Now, you have to realize that my dad had no idea I had not finished the patio. He hadn't been told nor could he see it. That's when I realized that he was again fighting against leaving us. I thought to myself that his spirit could see the things yet to be done and believe me, the hairs on my body stood to full attention at this. I looked at him and said, "Ok, Daddy, I'll finish today."

I had many thoughts that day and one was that if I didn't finish my dad wouldn't leave us. I know that sounds crazy but with everything else we had experienced during this season, I believed that anything was possible. As I cleaned, repotted, cleaned some more, and put things away tears were streaming down my face. I prayed and spoke to Jesus that day. "Jesus, I thank You for keeping my father here for this amazing year, but I still don't want him to leave. Please give me strength to bear what comes ahead." I felt a load lift as I moved bricks, and then after all was done, I sat on the steps of the patio with my chin in my hands and wondered if this was the last day I would see my father.

The next morning, I told my dad that the patio was complete. It probably was not as good as he would have it but I had done my best at putting things away and cleaning it up. He thanked me and we ate breakfast together. After that, my father never mentioned the patio again. I fed my dad pudding and some protein drink for his breakfast. After we were done, I sat on my mom's bed and we reminisced about all our happy family times. It was a beautiful day and as we sat there enjoying each other's company I pulled the curtain to the patio, letting some sunlight in. A visitor had hopped up the steps and sat on the top step peering through the big sliding glass door.

"A rabbit, Mom, look," I said.

To this day I am tickled at this God incident. Truly this was another gift for our time together.

As the rabbit peered in, I knew that this visit was a measure of comfort and joy for my mother. Now I must add that neither up to that day nor since have I witnessed a small wild bunny hop up a steep flight of brick stairs off a cement patio. There were no goodies or snacks to be had on the stairs that would have attracted such a sweet visitor. I do know that we sure did enjoy our visitor that day. For a few moments we were distracted by the sweet miracle of God's creation and thanked the Lord for His sweetness!

This rabbit's visit gave my mother something more to share, more memories. My mother was always fond of rabbits and had rabbit figurines around the house and now I knew why. She told me that during her youth my grandfather raised rabbits. Grandfather Knapik raised rabbits! Oh, how much fun, I thought, as my mother shared. She must have enjoyed those rabbits. Now Mom told me he didn't raise them because they were cute and cuddly or to have as pets. My grandfather raised them to feed his family of six and I am sure he used the fur somehow, because the Knapik family was not wasteful. They were immigrants from Czechoslovakia and took nothing for granted.

How amazing is God, that during my father's time of waiting, during our many hours of waiting, He would utilize every moment for insight into His love. It is wonderful how God uses our waiting to provide opportunities to be thankful. We can see the good rather than focus on the bad of a situation.

Recently, my son applied to colleges across our beautiful state of Virginia. His number one pick is an extremely difficult school to get into. He has all the qualities and characteristics as well as the grades to get into this prestigious school but so do a large percentage of the other thousands of kids that apply. The waiting to hear is gut wrenching and grueling at best. This wait tries every bit of patience. His application was deferred, meaning we have to wait another few months to know if he will be attending this school. So, I will continue waiting, but this time I will intentionally give it all to the Lord and not check constantly to see if we've heard yet. But let me also say that it was a sorrow to this momma's heart that he wasn't accepted yet, because as my son's mom I desire for him to get what he desires when I know it is good.

Our Father in heaven is much the same and so much better and wiser. He wants good things for us. I believe it grieves Him when we pine for things that are not good for us. As a mother or father can see that some choices have negative results, so our heavenly Father sees when we are heading in the wrong direction. Many times we are not willing to wait and be patient for the good or better things. Even more we forget to put God into our vision or goals. I believe when we put God first in our vision and goals, the choices become clearer.

As I reflect on patience and waiting it seems to me that sometimes we set ourselves up for frustration and failure through desiring instant gratification, succumbing to impulse buys. Our world is full of temptations to those traps and sets us up as well. We can get into big trouble or a heart full of hurt when we grab hold of the temporary rather than the eternal. This earth is a temporary home. We are just visiting vessels here to emit God's grace and love. We should allow Jesus to shine through our words and actions.

God prepares us for everything we experience. He even assists us in the waiting by giving us His Word and promises.

Now, let me tell you about me; I am an impulsive person. I love living life, experiencing the highs. But being impulsive has so many drawbacks. It doesn't allow the Word of God to permeate our thoughts and actions. And allowing the natural inclination to impulsiveness can lead to some lows.

I don't much like the lows in life, whether self-inflicted as a natural consequence of my actions or words, or those that just happen, like rejection, or the death of my father.

We all experience lows, whether we are impulsive or patient. During these times we need to recognize that God is still there for His children.

He doesn't remove the lows; but God can and does walk with us through them, through the power of the Holy Spirit.

We go through these seasons, but as followers of Christ we go through them knowing that with God we will get through. Philippians 4:13 says that through Christ who strengthens us, we can do all things. He desires us to walk through those situations, yet so many times we attempt to self-medicate, push down the hurt, run away from the season, or just grow numb. I propose we walk through the season, no matter how difficult it is. Walk through it knowing that every step is a step closer to the good, to God's glory.

> When I walk through difficult times now I attempt to see what God is doing, instead of what I am feeling.

It was during the painful waiting that God worked in my life and still does. I used to call it the "hammer," a push in the right direction or a nudge that wakes me up. When I walk through difficult times now I attempt to see what God is doing, instead of what I am feeling. As I finish this book, I have been bombarded with physical, emotional, and mental trials and challenges. Most of the time I seek God to get through, but honestly, sometimes I still find myself relying on old thoughts or habits. I pray continually that those old thoughts and habits will leave, but the first steps are waiting on God, being in His Word consistently, and being patient. So, for you I pray that you would tap into God's Word, His promises, His sacrifice of Jesus on the cross, and His Holy Spirit to strengthen you and to lift you as you go through life's waiting times and seasons.

CHAPTER 8

MORE GOD INCIDENTS

> Now to him who is able to do immeasurably more than all we ask or imagine, according to his power that is at work within us, to him be glory in the church and in Christ Jesus throughout all generations, for ever and ever! Amen. (Ephesians 3:20–21)

As I draft this book, memories flood my mind. I did not go through life without bumps, bruises, and some big challenges, but I was blessed to have a family that taught me the love of Jesus. Two flawed yet amazing parents sharing God's love with their children provided the platform I launched off into adulthood. I worked for many years with children who did not know the love of their own families, much less recognize the love of God. Being in the public school environment I was not afforded the luxury of teaching the children about God's great love for us. I did have the honor of living out His love daily, whether I felt like it or not. I prayed every morning to be led by the Holy Spirit and have the energy for whatever challenges came that day.

Near the end of the 2003 school year, I had to leave for a time to take care of my father. I was then teaching middle school students. This was one of my favorite groups of students and included a few kids that even now I still hear from occasionally. Luckily, during this specific year at the alternative school, I had an amazing partner who was able to carry the weight for the last two months of school. He was one of the most dependable and loyal people I ever had the privilege of working with.

The students would send me notes of encouragement. These students, whom many had "forgotten," continued to uplift my family and me during those challenging days. I was inspired by their love and kindness reflected in the cards they would send. To this day, I believe, and I pray they are working hard, knowing that they have a worthwhile contribution to make in the world. My heart overflows with memories of how God used these overlooked and forgotten children as channels of His love.

It was a tough year, but I knew that no one would be given more than they could handle, although my dad laughed about this statement every time it was mentioned. During this time with my father, I was given much from the Lord. Years before I had told a dear friend, coworker, and PE teacher, Mr. Joseph, "I don't know what I'd do if anything ever happened to my parents. There is no way I could survive." He sweetly responded with, "Kelly, you are stronger than you know, and God will equip you if He brings you to such a place." I will never forget his sweet, encouraging words. He always had a way of speaking life into situations. He made an impact on my life and I was forever benefiting from his faith-filled conversations and encouragement. Many years later how profound and true his words became as God equipped me to deal with the devastation that my dad's illness brought. The example Mr. Joseph gave in faith became one more support in the journey of my personal relationship with Jesus.

As we go through life, what do we look at? Do we look at the problem or the way through?

As we go through life, what do we look at? Do we look at the problem or the way through? In John 14:6, Jesus says, "I am the way, the truth, and the life. No one comes to the Father except through me." What does that mean? Well, for me it means that I can rest assured that when I am brought to a place where I don't see a "way," God will show me that way because I trust in Jesus and He is the Way! Now, I realize if you're a believer you are agreeing with me right now, but what if you don't realize this truth? Ask God to show you!

It is not the "way" of the world, the easy route, or a trouble-free zone, nor is it a way around the circumstance or challenge. I eventually did have to face my father's death, but my dad was given the miracle of living for longer than the doctors had predicted, and all credit for that goes to God! He answered my specific, faith-filled prayer. God answered Dad's daughter's prayer for an extension on his life, that the cancer would leave long enough for him to have an impact on his grandson.

God had an impact on all of us through this season. And that was the greatest miracle of all. Faith in Jesus as "the Way" has many challenges, but when we know the truth about who Christ is and what He did for us, these challenges become less critical. We realize who we are in Christ. Our identity is found in Jesus, and this relieves us of questioning who we are. We know that in Christ we can overcome because He overcame!

The Bible gives us the tools we need to find "the Way." But you can't find Jesus if you aren't willing to look! So many times, Christians are relying on a crutch rather than seeing what truths the Bible holds. In my younger years praying was something I did all the time. I prayed and prayed, especially when I needed something. I would hold Mass in my bedroom because I loved to be in God's presence.

When I opened my Bible for the first time in my late twenties, I began to grow in wisdom, knowledge, faith, and love. That last word, love, was much easier when I was a child. That is what Jesus meant in Matthew 18:2–4 when He said that we must become like little children to enter His kingdom. To love as a child means to take out judgment, labels, opinions, and more things that block or taint our love as adults. It means to have a love that is pure. As I age, I continue to find it difficult to deal with some people, much less love them. Yet in God's Word I learned that it is those very people God has called us to love. We don't need to agree with people to love them. Thankfully, God, in His infinite mercy and grace, has shown us what it looks like to love. He sent His only Son, Jesus, to be betrayed, rejected, berated, spat upon, beaten, whipped, and hung on a cross to die. Love looks like that? Yes, it means that we are willing to put aside our comfort and what we want in exchange for what God wants. Wow! God's love is the Real Deal, and His love covers a multitude of sins and our selfish motives, desires, and hang-ups.

As I pondered this chapter, a strong revelation from God came to me. We must not doubt God! I encourage you, dear reader, to understand that God always knows, and He always cares! God can and will do what we cannot even imagine!

Can we visit heaven before our death? Yes, I believe God allows it and does it! Who am I to limit God's ways and purposes? Many a story has been shared about journeys to heaven and each one shares such wonder and excitement. Do I think God allows intervention when someone is dying? Yes! Do I know that God will utilize things outside our understanding? Yes! There are so many stories that my father shared as he was departing this life. Many of them are remembered in this book. The following story is another example of how awesome God is. He loves us and desires for us to know the hidden things!

One evening my father awoke from a doze. He told my mom and me that his mother, who had died at childbirth, had come with his Aunt Rena, who was also deceased, to get him. He stated that my Aunt Rena was not happy with him because he would not leave with them. Then he began talking with us about Tom. When we asked who Tom was, my dad responded, "My little brother." Then Dad fell asleep again. My mom and I were wondering whom my father was referring to. Dad had two sisters and no brothers. So, we called his sister, my Aunt Jane, and conveyed the story. She began to cry. My mother and I both had a phone as we listened to my Aunt Jane share who she believed Tom to be.

Aunt Jane said that their mother had died during her pregnancy and never delivered the baby. To that very day they never knew if their sibling was a boy or a girl. My dad's little brother, Tom, was this baby. My own mother was speechless when contemplating this very idea. But we thought we would ask Dad about it again when he woke up.

When my dad woke up, he said again that his mother had come to bring him home and brought his little brother, Tom. We asked him who Tom was and he said again it was his brother. When he further talked about this, he said that it was his brother who died along with his mother while she was in labor.

WOW, what a sweet revelation. My dad had a brother in heaven; I have another uncle in heaven. What joy God gives even at the end of our lives!

Now, let me say again that I know that this is not something everyone will believe, nor do you need to. I do know that it gave my aunt a sense of peace about her mother and brother. It also gave us all a sense that we serve an awesome and amazing God who wants to give us more than we can fathom.

As I wrote this book, I realized that there would be many things that people may not understand, that I still did not fully understand. My job was not to convince myself or anyone else but to share what God had shared with me through the Holy

Spirit and God's Word. And in this book through my father's words, I'm doing just that, as honestly and authentically as I can. This book started with a story of what God shared; it is now so much more. It is a testimony to the love and mercy of a Father who desires His children to come home.

God doesn't need us to defend Him! Through Jesus Christ, God has already won! He desires us to desire Him, to be in relationship with Him. Have you decided yet? Have you accepted Jesus Christ as your Savior? Be on the lookout—if you have answered the call and accepted Jesus Christ as your redeemer, God will shower you with sweet blessings leading you to more insight of God's love, mercy, and grace. If you have not asked Jesus into your heart, be on the lookout and listen. God is calling you to know and follow Him through the gate—His Son, Jesus Christ, the Good Shepherd.

Jesus tells us in John 10:1–18:

> "Very truly I tell you Pharisees, anyone who does not enter the sheep pen by the gate, but climbs in by some other way, is a thief and a robber. The one who enters by the gate is the shepherd of the sheep. The gatekeeper opens the gate for him, and the sheep listens to his voice. He calls his own sheep by name and leads them out. When he has brought out

all his own, he goes on ahead of them, and his sheep follow him because they know his voice. But they will never follow a stranger; in fact, they will run away from him because they do not recognize a stranger's voice." Jesus used this figure of speech, but the Pharisees did not understand what he was telling them.

Therefore, Jesus said again, "Very truly I tell you, I am the gate for the sheep. All who have come before me are thieves and robbers, but the sheep have not listened to them. I am the gate; whoever enters through me will be saved. They will come in and go out and find pasture. The thief comes only to steal and kill and destroy; I have come that they may have life, and have it to the full.

"I am the good shepherd. The good shepherd lays down his life for the sheep. The hired hand is not the shepherd and does not own the sheep. So, when he sees the wolf coming, he abandons the sheep and runs away. Then the wolf attacks the flock and scatters it. The man runs away because he is a hired hand and cares nothing for the sheep.

> "I am the good shepherd; I know my
> sheep and my sheep know me—just as
> the Father knows me and I know the
> Father—and I lay down my life for the
> sheep. I have other sheep that are not
> of this sheep pen. I must bring them
> also. They too will listen to my voice,
> and there shall be one flock and one
> shepherd. The reason my Father loves
> me is that I lay down my life—only
> to take it up again. No one takes it
> from me, but I lay it down of my own
> accord. I have authority to lay it down
> and authority to take it up again. This
> command I received from my Father."

Jesus states that He is the Gate and He is the Good
Shepherd. Those who hear His voice know it. My
hope and prayer is that you hear the voice of the
Good Shepherd and enter through Him. God desires us to come, all of us! He's not willing to leave
one behind but it is totally up to you. Are you willing
to answer? It takes a total surrender of yourself to
God and a total trust in knowing that God is FOR
REAL AND FOR YOU! He loves you! When
you experience God's love, everything begins! It is
a new beginning, small steps and big steps, but the
entire time God has you and is not willing to lose
you. He will continue to prompt, guide, discipline,

and always in love, a love that is pure. May God bless you as you continue to seek Him in every area of your life! Look out for the God incidents; they are all around you waiting for you to see!

CHAPTER 9

THE GRAND BUFFETT

> When one of those at the table with Him heard this, he said to Jesus, "Blessed is the one who will eat at the feast in the kingdom of God." (Luke 14:15)

Close to the end of my father's days on this earth he began speaking to my mother and me about a great feast. He referred to this feast as a "grand buffet." "Kelly, you wouldn't believe it unless you saw it. It's a grand buffet. Everyone is there at the table." As we sat and listened to my father talking to us about the endless feast and the many people that were there, we began to be excited over my dad's excitement about where he was going. He would be at a feast in the kingdom of God. Nothing compares to his description, and let me tell you that my dad knew buffets; he knew where to go to get the best meals. He said the meal itself was grand but there was "so much more" than my mother or I could imagine, and my dad was able to see it and share it. WOW, another God gift! I praised God for again giving my mother and me peace about where Daddy was going and for giving us a glimpse at where we would meet again. To say that this was just a story would be to limit what God wanted us to know. This experience was part of the Real Deal. Knowing that there is a place at the great feast in the kingdom of God for all those who believe brings hope into my heart for all.

Recently, my husband and I were visiting churches in the Outer Banks of North Carolina, where we plan to be full-time next year. At one of the local churches, Liberty, I listened intently to another amazing sermon. The assistant pastor was speaking about seats around the table in heaven. He said, "There's a seat with your name on it; no one else can sit in it and yet there are many empty seats." Personally, I'd like every seat filled and every person saved. What about you? Would you like to be at this Grand Buffet?

In Scripture, the breaking of bread and sharing of a meal was a time of coming together, honoring God, and enjoying fellowship. Jesus, before being arrested and dying on the cross, shared a meal with His disciples. Many churches continue this tradition, referring to it as Communion. We take Communion as a remembrance of what Jesus did for us. He sacrificed His body, His life, so that we could have eternal life in heaven. He is the ultimate sacrifice, tearing the veil that kept us from having a relationship with Father God. He is the Bread of

Life and the Cup of Salvation. Anyone who believes in Jesus will have eternal life and sit at the table of this feast. A place has been prepared for all those who believe.

The Old Testament of the Bible (before Jesus) is filled with how the Israelites were to atone for sins prior to Jesus the Messiah's coming. Sacrifices, the offerings you brought, were made at the altar by a High Priest to atone for your sins. Jesus became the unblemished sacrifice for all humanity so that we could come to the Father. Because of what Jesus did, nothing can separate you from the love of the Father. Nothing can stand in the way of that relationship. The only way is Jesus. God willingly gave His only Son, Jesus Christ, so that we might come to Him, believe, and have eternal life. Jesus Christ was and is the Real Deal!

There is only one thing standing in the way of our union with Father God and that is us! We have free will, the ability to choose. We can choose to live our lives without this relationship and find other sources of temporary satisfaction but there is only one way that we will be satisfied with everlasting benefits, and that way is Jesus. Nothing else can permanently benefit you the way that a relationship with God can. Believe me, for years I tried everything to fill spaces and find answers that would bring wholeness and peace. God lovingly forgave me and when I finally came to the full knowledge of Jesus, it changed my life forever. Some of the change was hard. Friends I had known most of my life faded when I began my relationship with Christ. Sometimes that happens. In fact, I can remember a time when I had no friends. But what was amazing is that as I pressed into God and sat with Him daily, He began to bring new friends into my life who shared a passion for His kingdom and ways. My life is much different now, but I have no regrets about friends lost because I know that God loves them just as much as He loves me, and He will find ways to reach them too.

Another fact that I want you to know is that you are special. God has already chosen you! He sent His Son, Jesus, to die for you. So never question "if" God wants a relationship with you. I am reminding you He does. Nothing that you have done can change that. Jesus was the reparation for all the sin in the world, and we know that sin exists. We know that we have sinned. Jesus asks us to repent of that life of sin and accept His forgiveness and allow Him to personally become our Lord and Savior.

Many people are good, according to our judgment of good and bad, but good people still need Jesus to receive absolution for sin. Jesus our Savior brings us to the table of the feast of our Father God. Don't be fooled into thinking that anyone is naturally good enough. None of us is good enough and that is why Jesus came. We have been purchased for a price. The purchase was to keep us out of hell; the price was Jesus coming to earth, to be fully man and to die on a cross for us. The only way to stay out of hell is to accept the gift of Jesus Christ's sacrifice. There is no way to earn your spot in heaven; you must be in relationship with Jesus.... That's why He came.

If you had told me years ago that I would be authoring a book I would have said yes. I always enjoyed writing. If you had said I would be writing a book about Jesus and that He is the only way to the Father ... I wouldn't have agreed. I had part of the picture as a churched youngster, even as a teenager. I knew that I believed but wouldn't share the truth with others because I hadn't yet submitted or surrendered to God. I lived my life, my way. It wasn't until God began to reveal Himself to me through His Word and many amazing friends in faith that I understood what faith as a follower of Christ looked like.

So, would I have said I would write about Jesus at that time? No. In fact, there were people I ran from because they were such "Jesus Freaks." I'd run to the drunks, the partiers, the fun, but, "Don't be telling me how to live my life and that my friends were going to hell because they didn't know the Lord." That's how I saw things at that time. I lived through many incidents that led me to my knees praying for contentment, wisdom, and love. God answered all those prayers and my faith has gradually grown. This growth is still in process and will be, until my Father God calls me to my heavenly home.

I have written *The Real Deal* out of obedience, not choice! I have many times, much like Jonah, run from finishing it but God continually calls me back. He reiterates His desire for me to complete this project. The Holy Spirit continues to prompt me to finish this work. This is His work! If I do not complete this book, it will be a matter of disobedience to the Lord. I confess, I have been disobedient in this process. I start strong and then somewhere in the process I get scared.... I'm not sure of what, but that is the honest truth, coming from this woman who loves the Lord with all her heart!

God has already completed His work. Jesus said before He died on the cross, "It is finished" (see John 19:30). Oh, that we would see the finished work of Jesus and come to know Him.

My father was the kind of man who loved all-you-can-eat buffets. When my husband, Jim, and I were dating, we went to Ohio to visit family with my mother and father. Our family bonding times were spent catching up and almost always eating. We went for breakfast at Old Country Buffet, one of our family's favorites. There we spent three hours eating and catching up. My dad drank coffee, at least two pots of it. It was a sight to see; my husband, Jim, still laughs as he revisits that memory because my dad left such an impression on him. He couldn't believe Dad could sit and drink coffee for hours. My father enjoyed times with good food, hot coffee, and dear family and friends. He enjoyed listening to stories and laughing. So, for him to reflect on heaven and call what was there "a grand buffet," it had to be something spectacular. It is!

What is heaven like? That's one of the things I wanted to know. I prayed early on in my father's illness that I would know where he was going and that I would have reassurance of this. In fact, I can remember praying to God and asking Him for this reassurance. I told my parents that if there was any way for them to let me know they were okay to please do that. Sounds silly now to think about it based on what I know, but I believe that God desires to bless us in and through tragic events. He doesn't want to see us hurt or hurting. In fact, His original creation had none of that. But when sin entered the world so did the pain and suffering that it caused.

> We know that in all things God works for the good of those who love him, who have been called according to his purpose. (Romans 8:28)

This is a difficult verse to understand when we are faced with unthinkable tragedies, but there are a few key words I reflect on to help me through those times. First, "We know...." Oh, Lord, please let me know; I want to know! Second, "all things"; not just some things, but, in all things, no matter what our thoughts are on a situation or our feelings, faith in God matters most here. We need to know in all things. The prophet Jeremiah is a great one to reflect on to understand how we are to know.... The Lord told him in Jeremiah 33:1–3 who He was and what Jeremiah needed to do to know the mighty hidden things. He told Jeremiah to "call to me, and I will answer you, and tell you great and mighty things" (NKJV). God is the same God to us that He was to Jeremiah. He desires that we would call on Him. God will answer and show us the things that we need to know! Don't doubt because you are going through a tough time. Get on your knees and cry out to God! Talk to Him. Ask Him specific things. He will answer; be patient. And lastly, don't be discouraged when God says no, or doesn't answer the way you want. The "yes" He has is better than what you could ask or imagine. So don't be distracted or pulled down into despair. Call out to Father God, ask Him, and He will answer!

When tragedy strikes, looking at the good and encouraging is not easy. In fact, it takes supernatural help from the Holy Spirit to look at the bright side. I imagine Jesus Himself stayed on the cross, enduring the pain and suffering of sin, for the bright side, that we would be able to enter heaven and sit with Him at this great feast. He loves us all so much. He wants us to be at the table with Him in heaven. I want to be at the table with Him when I am called home.

So, it is sweet, the vision of the "grand buffet" that my father shared, and it just warms my heart. I hope it encourages your heart too!

I remember sharing some of these moments with people who do not know the Lord and their comments were cerebral at best. One person said that my dad must have been "high." I will never forget that comment, but I had to forgive this dear person. I had to realize that everyone has their own thoughts and interpretations of what we experience. Before a person knows God, they are filled with the things of the world and worldly thinking. I pray that those who often have snap answers and utilize intellectual reasoning will be awakened to see all that God is and does. I have no doubt that before I understood Christ and salvation, I unknowingly made some ridiculous comments that hurt others. In fact, I can assure you that I am not perfect even now that I am saved. But I want you to know, as you read this, that my father was not "high" or just on good pain killers. He was experiencing the love, hope, and promise from God our Father through the power of the Holy Spirit. He probably wouldn't have described it as such, but seeing the work that God was doing in and through him during this challenging season blessed all those who were involved. From the hired caregivers and hospice to dear friends, coworkers, and family, God gave us all real insight to His abiding love and mercy and what we have awaiting us all as believers.

And I, along with others who visited or experienced these days with my dad, shared in the knowing. It is a knowing that God is who He says He is, that He answers prayers (even if it's not the way you asked), and that He is in the miracle business!

> You don't have to be perfect; God is the only perfection, and you are the work of His hands, wonderfully and fearfully made for a plan and a purpose.

Let's look further at Jeremiah 33:1–3, where God speaks to Jeremiah and tells him to "call to me, and I will answer you, and show you great and mighty things." These are the hidden things that we cannot see without the Lord. These hidden things God desires for us to know. Too often we just don't ask Him. Often we search in so many places looking to find the answers when God tells us repeatedly in the Bible to seek Him above all else. My advice to you would be to look for the miracles in your life. Look for the daily sweetness and the glimmerings of salvation. They are there and, yes, Jesus is the reason that they are! I praise God that He uses even that cutting comment made to me about my dad to draw me closer to others and share His love. Don't allow evil to make you think that God's blessings aren't real! God loves us so much that He is willing to utilize everything in order to shine the light and clear a path for us to see.

I pray that you can know this truth, that you hear God's voice calling you right now, and that your heart is open to receive Jesus into your life. You don't have to be perfect; God is the only perfection, and you are the work of His hands, wonderfully and fearfully made for a plan and a purpose (see Psalm 139:14; Jeremiah 29:11).

CHAPTER 10

THE NIGHT BEFORE

The evening before my father died, we talked past midnight. Dad had so much to say. He kept talking and talking. Looking back, he must have known in some way that he was leaving and that this would be our last conversation for a while. I can only say, from the time I was quite young until that evening before my dad died, my fondest memories were time spent in conversations with him. He always encouraged, sometimes disciplined, and always seemed to have the answers to life's complicated dilemmas.

After the diagnosis of cancer, my dad and I never let a visit go by without a conversation to send me on my way home. Every time I went by the house Dad would walk me to my car and we'd spend an extra twenty minutes or so just chitchatting. In many ways these days between diagnosis and death were filled with lessons about life and I would later recall all the sweet discussions between my dad and me.

So, this last evening before his death was filled with conversation to the point that it had become excruciatingly late, into the early morning hours, and my mother finally said, "Jack, Kelly needs her sleep and so do you." Well, at my mother's request my father quickly summed up the conversation and I told him that we'd catch up the following day. Little did I know that we'd had our last real conversation. His last breaths wouldn't be used for spoken words. Oh, how I miss our talks!

After my mom urged my dad to get some sleep, he told me he loved me and wished me "sweet dreams." Then I prayed, and off to slumber we all went.

The night before He was put to death by crucifixion, Jesus prayed to His Father to take this cup (what was to happen) from Him. He prayed three times in Gethsemane that it be His Father's will, not His own, that should be done. Jesus repeatedly asked the disciples who were in the garden with Him to stay awake and pray. Jesus loved His disciples; they were like family. He asked them to stay awake and knew that they had to respond individually by either staying awake or falling asleep. The Gospels of Matthew, Mark, and Luke record this "night before" scene almost identically.

As I reflect on this part of Jesus's last night, I see a correlation with my dad's final night before death. Just maybe Dad knew his time was near and he wanted to stay awake. Had we known it would be his last night, we would have stayed awake with him. Instead, much like the disciples, we all went to sleep.

These accounts give us the words "keep watch" in multiple translations, or "watch" in the King James Version. The phrases "keep watch" or "watch" are also spoken by Jesus in Matthew 24:42 after His resurrection. In fact, in the English Standard Version of the Bible, Jesus states, "Therefore, stay awake, for you do not know on what day your Lord is coming." I can't speak for you, but I sure want Jesus to know I have prepared for Him by truly surrendering my life to His Lordship and will for me. This surrender, repentance, and confession that Jesus is Lord of my life is the only way my salvation is guaranteed. I believe that keeping watch involves prayer, supplication, and staying true to God's infallible Word, the Bible. In order to stay true to His Word, we must know it. In other words, we must know Jesus if we are to live our lives as reflections of Him. We won't live perfectly, as Jesus did, but we'll do the best we can, with heartfelt longing to keep Him as our focal point.

As I was sleeping in the same room near my mom, I awakened to my dad's rapid breathing. It was unlike anything I had ever heard before. It scared me! Even knowing that my dad was outside heaven's gate and that his pain would cease once he passed, I still was not prepared for this stage of his passing. I quickly made all the necessary calls and rushed to his side along with my mom. She held his hand and we prayed, sang, and cried as my dad struggled to breathe. He was awake and he saw us, but he couldn't speak. It was as if all his strength and focus were on taking the next breath, with no extra energy to talk. My husband knew, when the time came for my dad's passing, how difficult it would be for us. Being true to how wonderful he is, he showed up to say goodbye to my dad and support us in any way he could. This day, June 24, was our third wedding anniversary. It made this day bittersweet, but it would be just like my dad to leave on such a wonderful day so we would not mourn years after his departure.

Until my dad's sister, Aunt Mary, arrived from Cleveland, we clung to my dad's every breath. As my Aunt Mary Krause was en route from the airport, I realized that it was also nearing the exact time of my wedding ceremony. How poignant that I would celebrate my marriage and my dad's parting at the same time. Something inside told me to let him know that it was okay, that indeed I would celebrate this day even though he was leaving. I knew he understood. I hoped this would be one of the many things that would ease his parting.

My dad always thought about everyone else. His exterior was impenetrable but inside he had a heart of compassion for others. His love for my mother, brother, and me was in proportion to the love he had for others. He wouldn't express it in words, but he always looked out for the underdog and wanted others to be happy. This day was no different. He was in pain, but he didn't want to leave. He especially didn't want to leave my mom. Jim, my husband, reassured him one last time that my mother and I would be fine. He would see to it! Still, my dad loved my mom so much. He just couldn't figure out how life would look or work without him there to take care of her. He was the one who provided and made sure everything ran efficiently. He fixed everything, took care of the bills, and knew that my mom's health was deteriorating. This was a nightmare to him, and as optimistic as he tried to be about all things, this was really stretching him. Much like I expect Job in the Bible felt, he couldn't wrap his head or heart around the "why" and "how" of the situation. Not "why me," just "why."

When my Aunt Mary arrived, she immediately took his hand, telling him, "It's okay, Jack, you can go now." As we pushed away the tears that welled up in our eyes, Mom and I also told him that it was okay to go. At that point, my dad looked directly at my mom and took his last breath. That breath was a slow one compared to the fast pace that we had seen all morning. It was his final goodbye. I will never forget the peace on his face, and the atmosphere was so sweet. I was in shock, but there was a peace. Peace that he didn't have to suffer any longer. Peace in knowing that at that very moment, he was in heaven with Jesus.

I cannot even begin to describe to you how emotional I am about many things; I believe "passionate" is an accurate term. No matter how attached or detached you are on the emotional scale, watching someone you love die is one of the most traumatic life events you will ever experience. You don't want them to leave, plain and simple. Even when you are reassured about their destination, you have so much difficulty in the letting go.

When I hear people say, "It's only by God's grace," I think back to letting go of my dad. *Challenging* isn't even a good descriptor for what those who are left behind must endure. Yet we must go on! Move forward! Many times, when you lose a loved one you just want the whole world to stop and take notice. You desire a pause out of respect for your loved one. Statistically, if there was a halt every time someone passed, we'd be pausing so much the universe would never move! Yes, I do like to think about these deep concepts; a passionate deep thinker am I!

Now I want you to imagine someone giving their child's life to save the lives of everyone who will ever live. Are you wondering why someone would give their child's life for all mankind? Maybe they know that the only way for humanity to live fully alive now and eternally is to give their only child. What if that was your child? Wouldn't you want people to know that they live because of the sacrifice of your child? Wouldn't you want people to join you in praise and honor for that debt that was paid by your child's death? Jesus Christ, son of Mary and Joseph, did just that!! Born in Bethlehem, died on Calvary's cross, and risen from that death three days later. God gave His only Son, Jesus, to be the atonement for all sin. He desired that no one should perish but that all would have everlasting life with Him in heaven.

I'm just saying, if you haven't thought about the price that was paid for your eternal life, now is the time! We all will come before the Lord God Almighty and give an account for our own life. I assume the first question will be, "Do you believe in Jesus Christ, My only Son, who died to set you free?" The answer to this question right now sets your eternity in place. You either believe or you don't.

There's no checklist of what good things you've done or how good you are. God's acceptance actually has nothing to do with how "good" you are. It has everything to do with knowing how amazing God is! It has everything to do with knowing He sent His only Son, Jesus Christ, to be born of a virgin, live with all the challenges of being human, and yet live without sinning. He was the only one who could be the perfect sacrifice. Jesus was the only one who could pay for all our sin. He was despised and rejected, challenged and tempted in every way humanly and spiritually possible, and led to die a sinner's death on a cross. Luckily, that is not the end of Jesus's story; it is the beginning of our redemption. Jesus's last words on the cross were, "It is finished." He had completed the race in His earthen vessel, His body, and miraculously the next time people would see Jesus walk again would be after He had been dead for three days!

I don't know you personally, but I know God does. I know God loves you with a love that is pure and that is all encompassing. God desires a relationship with you and He desired you so much that He was willing to take the punishment for

> Being good is not good enough, but knowing God through His Son, Jesus, is!

the sin in each of us on His Son's body. Jesus loves you so much that He calls out to you and wants you to recognize and honor Him for who He is and for what has been done in order that you have eternal life. Being good is not good enough, but knowing God through His Son, Jesus, is!

God's love for us is the Real Deal, and as I have written, I pray you will come to know Jesus Christ, the unblemished Lamb who took your sins away. Jesus did not grow weary for loving you; He stayed on the cross bearing all burdens without calling for His rescue. Oh, how I pray you know His love!

CHAPTER 11

LETTING GO

The Lord is my shepherd, I shall not want. He makes me lie down in green pastures; He leads me beside quiet waters. He restores my soul. (Psalm 23:1–3a NASB)

*L*ord, You are my provider, and You give me every-thing that I need. I will not be in want. I will be in hope of what You have prepared for me this moment, this day! For my days are numbered on this earth and as I live and breathe, I will give it all to You!

It has been over twenty years since my dad's last breath. I made it through his last breath and lost my mother less than a year after my dad. I knew after my father died that I was supposed to be a witness of heaven's reality and the goodness God has for those who love Him (see Romans 8:12). To share and tell people about what I had experienced, my testimony. I knew that God was calling me; what I did not know is that it would take me this long to "let go."

When I began this chapter many years ago, it was about my dad, his letting go. Today as I type out these words, I realize that God had more in store for me than the story of what we look forward to when we leave this earth as followers of Jesus Christ. He wanted me to make people aware of His love and His Son's promised return. When He told me to write *The Real Deal*, as you recall I was in Bible study and He gave me that title. So, what does it mean to let go and what is the Real Deal?

It means letting go of everything we hold on to and that holds on to us. Brothers and sisters, I do not consider myself to have taken hold of it. But one thing I do: forgetting what is behind and reaching forward to what is ahead, I pursue as my goal the prize promised by God's heavenly call in Christ Jesus (see Philippians 3:13–14 CSB).

> Forgetting what is behind and reaching forward to what is ahead.

Jesus Christ is the Real Deal. We must let go of our feelings and reasonings and understand what God says. The only way to know what God says is to read and study the Bible! This is the only truth; I can't make up the stories or the words that our Father in heaven inspired the writers of the Bible to write. I can tell you though that the Bible is life-giving, living, breathing.... In essence it is what will propel us from being Sunday-only Christians to followers of Christ. It is the most powerful tool we will ever need, and we must utilize it. Much like our bodies require food, water, and oxygen, so the spirit that lives inside us needs God's Word to replenish what our situations can attempt to take away: Faith, Hope, Love.

When you live in the world and of the world, you fall prey to the devil's schemes, and Satan wants nothing less than to keep you away from your God-given potential. Many times, Satan will keep you focused on the problems rather than the Solver. We need our Savior Jesus Christ, and the Bible gives us firsthand accounts of Jesus and His teachings.

We must let go of our preconceived notions about everything, let go of our judgments, our pride, our selfishness, our humanness, everything. God wants to fill us up with the Real Deal, Living Water, Holy Spirit, Eternal Life.

If I were to have a coupon and on it was printed, "TICKET TO LIVE FOREVER IN LOVE AND PEACE, ALL INCLUSIVE," would you take it, would you desire it, or would you pass it up? Now if that ticket also read PAID IN FULL and the only thing that you needed to do was to acknowledge that payment and receive the gift, wouldn't you want it?

People are buying products that promise what cannot be given—the fountain of youth—and yet salvation, freedom, and eternal life are free!!! The choice seems obvious, but many costly counterfeits come into our lives to distract us from the free gift of salvation. The devil has come to steal, kill, and destroy (see John 10:10)—make no mistake about that. Satan twists what God wants for you and makes it look bad or attempts to confuse you into thinking bad is good and good is bad. Let me remind you, there is no darkness in God (see 1 John 1:5). Don't allow Satan to rob you of the beauty and life that awaits those who live in Christ Jesus.

What acknowledgment do we need to make? That Jesus is the Son of God, that He suffered, died, was buried, and rose from the dead. During the Last Supper before Jesus was taken and put to death, He spoke to His disciples and told them, "I am the way, the truth, and the life. No one comes to the Father except through me" (John 14:6).

I believe that gives some understanding of why it is so important to let go of our false ideologies and come to understand that Jesus is the Real Deal. Jesus came as our ticket to our prepared eternal paradise. The Bible is the most powerful tool we have to see paradise here on earth. God's Word is full of promises and guidance. Why wouldn't we accept it?

God's promises do not fall void; they bring life to the lifeless, healing to the broken, and love and comfort to the hurting.

Take a chance on God, invest your time in His Word, and come to know the Real Deal of Jesus Christ. I promise, He will never let you down and you will never go hungry. Through Christ you will combat fear, rejection, loneliness, confusion—all these and more. These are attacks that come straight from the pit of hell. Call on Jesus and the devil has to flee. Remember, Jesus is the Way and in God there is no darkness, so seek the light of the world and let go of all that has made you weary or heavy burdened. God gives rest!

You may have a lot to let go of a lot, you may have a little, but we all have something we need to let go of and let God in. Since God is in it all already, let God help you realize that through Christ you can do all things (see Philippians 4:13).

CHAPTER 12

MAKING A DEAL

You may remember that in chapter seven I mentioned my father mumbling something about a "deal" he had made with God. At the time, I didn't know what to make of his words, and I still don't believe that there was anything more to the "deal" than my dad pleading God to take care of his wife and children, but it was something that we chuckled over during the last days of my father's life on earth.

In Benny Hinn's book, *Good Morning, Holy Spirit*, Hinn refers to it not being unusual for people who were raised in his culture to "bargain" with God. Until I read this amazing book, I thought it was foolish to think that my dad had really made a "deal" with God. Still, I pondered the thought of "bargaining" with God and "making deals" with our Father in heaven. I first thought about how we as children like to bargain with our parents and attempt to get what we want with as little effort as possible. It's a pleading, "Please, Daddy, please, I'll be good." Sometimes it's, "Please, Daddy, please, I'll do whatever you need me to do" (clean my room, take out the trash, mow the lawn, etc.). As children we are completely absorbed in the pleading; we completely desire what we are pleading for. We are relentless as children when we desire something.

I remember pleading with God many times as a child that those who were suffering would no longer suffer. I was an extremely compassionate child and remember thinking on many things that were close to God's heart. When others hurt, I hurt for them. I also pleaded with my parents, especially if it had to do with animals coming into the house. I loved animals and they always had a way of finding me. I believe my home had a "Stray Animals Welcome" sign on it. My parents, on the other hand, were not always so excited about this sign and sometimes it took a little more pleading to house the latest stray.

In my father's case, his pleading was never about him. He was always thinking of his family, and during the last few years of his life he was mainly thinking about my mother, her well-being, and her quality of life. I believe it frustrated and saddened him when he was no longer able to care for her and he fought hard to stay alive and remain actively participating in daily life. Once he was for the most part unable to physically engage, he would still have input and insights. Some of the most memorable moments of my life were spent at my father's bedside.

I can remember my dad telling me that he was "making a deal" with God. I laughed, but as I considered this, I thought about his desire for my mother to live and be well. He knew she was having increasing difficulty getting around and her balance and motor skills were diminishing more and more. She still had lots of love and grace; she just couldn't get around as well. God knows how painful that must have been for them both.

My dad's making a deal was like a prayer to God that his wife would be okay, that his children would be okay, and that without the patriarch of our earthly family we would continue to thrive. Wow, how much my dad loved us, though it doesn't compare to the love that God has for all of us.

I can compare the idea of my dad "making a deal" for his family's safety and flourishing to God "making a deal" to secure His children's futures. The difference is that God can actually "make a deal," offering us eternal joy and fellowship if we accept the gift of salvation through Jesus. God loves us all and His desire is that we would have a relationship with Him through His Son, Jesus Christ. Until we come to know the truth, it's as if God is at our side waiting for us to hear His voice and know His heart. I pray for so many that are lost and know that if you are reading this and you don't know Jesus, all you have to do is ask. Ask Jesus into your heart, repent of any sin, and get into the Holy Word of God—the Bible. I pray that people who know Christ's love would surround you and help you navigate being a follower of Jesus Christ. I support you in your pursuit of Jesus and encourage you to live daily for Christ.

Make a deal with yourself that every morning you will greet the Lord God as you step on the ground to start your day. You will know the Lord God through the power of the Holy Spirit who walks with you!

Can you make a deal with God? No. He has already sent the Real Deal, Jesus Christ, to bring us to eternal life with God, our Father in heaven. And Jesus is coming again, so be ready, filled with the love and hope of Christ!

CONCLUSION

My hope is that you, too, will be able to recognize the many God moments, incidents, and divine appointments that are sprinkled in your life throughout every day. Romans 8:28 says that God will work all things out for good. Do we believe? There is no blessing without the cross. Jesus Christ died and was resurrected so that we may live. So that all could come to God and be safe.

I forgave the people that stole something precious from me, traumatized me, and distorted my way of thinking and dealing with the world. I pray for those that hurt me in this way because I know how very much God loves them. I can only explain it like this. I want to see Jesus and His love for all people, not because of what they have done or do, but because of what Jesus has already done.

I realize there are many spaces in this story you may not understand, though I know that what you are meant to get out of it, you will. At the very least I have introduced you to my God, His Son, Jesus Christ, and the Holy Spirit, and how They've worked in my life turning ashes into beauty. Know

They can do more than what They've done for me. All you must do is ask, receive, and acknowledge. I'd like to end with a quote by Albert Einstein: "There are only two ways to live your life. One is as though nothing is a miracle. The other is as though everything is a miracle."[1]

Even in the worst of times I attempt to see everything (no exceptions) as a miracle based on God's Word, and more specifically in one of my favorite books of the Bible. Romans 8:28 states, "And we **know** that **all** things work together for good to those who love God, to those who are the called according to His purpose" (NKJV, emphasis mine). Sometimes it takes a while to see it as a miracle because the hurt can be so deep.

As believers in Jesus Christ, we are all called for His purpose. It's never too late and you're never too far gone to be saved. I have prayed for you, that you may have endurance to stand in your calling and in the unity of the Holy Spirit in love with all God's creation in order that Christ would be known.

The proceeds after the cost of printing this book you have purchased, or been gifted, have gone to Heart for the House, which will in turn give to those most in need through partnering with charities in the USA that reflect our mission to heal

---

1   "A Quote by Albert Einstein." Goodreads, 2023. https://www.goodreads.com/quotes/987-there-are-only-two-ways-to-live-your-life-one.

the hurting, give hope to the abandoned, and rescue the enslaved, turning lives around through the power and blessing of Jesus Christ.

IF YOU ENJOYED THIS BOOK, WILL YOU HELP ME SPREAD THE WORD?

There are several ways you can help me get the word out about the message of this book…

- Post a 5-Star review on Amazon.

- Write about the book on your Facebook, Twitter, Instagram, LinkedIn, – any social media you regularly use!

- If you blog, consider referencing the book, or publishing an excerpt from the book with a link back to my website. You have my permission to do this as long as you provide proper credit and backlinks.

- Recommend the book to friends – word-of-mouth is still the most effective form of advertising.

- Purchase additional copies to give away as gifts.

The best way to connect is by visiting:
kellydolanelhers.com